To my

My Great Grandmother Edith,
my m

My Great Grandmother Ruthy and Nicky, who I lost on
Sunday of the last week of December/early January.

To my fiancé Joseph, who I love more and more by the seconds.

To my old best friend Ryan Wagner, who also left us too soon.

To my niece Isabella Jade, who ran my world the day she was born.

My Grandparents, whose unconditional love made my life worth
every second.

I love you all.

*** This is a memoir, aka nonfiction. All of this is true and detailed to the best of my knowledge and capability of remembering. Names have been changed to protect the privacy of others. If you think you know someone, it might be because they remind you of someone in real life that isn't related to the person in this book. ***

Chapter One

I woke up confused. That wasn't unusual, but this morning something was off. Something didn't taste right. The phone was ringing off the hook, my father's bedroom door was shut, and the time on the television's clock read 7:15 A.M. I panicked automatically.

I was the young age of eight years old, chubby, with a dark mess of a bowl cut on my head. My mother was gone out of my life. Something about her being sick? I don't know. All I did know was that my momom and father came to some crazy agreement where I would live with him. I didn't like it. Momom was my life. She took care of me. She bathed me, fed me and tucked me in at night. Daddy only sometimes did all of those things. Why did they make me do this?

It didn't matter now. I rose up off the couch and literally tip-toed to his room. I remember my shaky, chubby hands opening the door and then closing them as soon as I saw his clothless body lying belly up. Why was he still asleep? Didn't he know it was Halloween? It was my 3rd grade Halloween Walk around the school; a new school at that! I had a costume and everything! Why is he still asleep?

The phone was blaring in my ear. I wasn't allowed to answer it for whatever reason. I didn't know what to do. I remember making the toilet flush repeatedly. I remember trying to make enough noise to wake him up with the one thought going through my head, "the water bill is going to be big, but he's gotta get up!" I put the TV all the way up to one hundred. That did nothing. I coughed really loudly by his room. That also did nothing. I started crying.

It wasn't an aggravated cry, either. It was an "I'm scared! Why isn't daddy waking up" cry. I had to answer the phone; that much was obvious. Fuck being in trouble! It's now 7:30 and my dad's not waking up.

I couldn't tell you my thoughts when I stepped towards that phone, and not just because I was only eight years old. I couldn't tell you my thoughts because of how horribly terrified I was. The caller ID said "New York" and although we were in Staten Island, the only person who's ID showed up as that was my other momom, my dad's mother. I cannot tell you how much of a fucking angel she sounded like. I cannot tell you how quickly I calmed down when I heard her voice.

"Kay...what's going on?" You could already tell in her voice she knew. Her worst fears came to life that day, just like mine did.

"Daddy won't wake up," I answered back. You could hear her breath hitch; how panic had set in. She calmly told me, however, that she would call me right back and I need to answer the phone. I hung up and waited, pacing around the small, linoleum tiled kitchen. I waited maybe half a minute for her to call back.
"Kayla, answer the door. Do you understand me?"
I said "yes", crying again when I heard how harsh her tone was. She was scared. I was scared and my own mother wasn't here to hug me and tell me it was okay.
"Aunt Erica and Grandma Edith are coming, okay? You open the door no matter what."

My Aunt Erica was my best friend, and Grandma Edith (actually my great grandmother) was in the same hierarchy as her. Obviously, they would make everything better. Obviously, they would somehow magically wake him up in ways a sobbing child could not.

When I tell you they came in five minutes, they probably came in three. They floored that car down Bloomingdale Road, making wide turns into my apartment complex that was White Oak Lane. I let them in and when they saw my face they ran past me into my father's room. I was too scared to move from my spot in the foyer.

It happened quickly after that. The screaming, the tears, the panicking.

"Craig!" my aunt screamed as she rushed passed my great grandmother who was doing the best CPR she could manage. My aunt screamed to 911. She hugged me then told me to run upstairs to my landlord's house so I wouldn't see the grisly scene of throw up and fear. My poor landlord's wife was in the middle of doing her child's Halloween makeup. When she heard my crying at the door, begging to be let in because my daddy wouldn't wake up, she let me right in.

When the ambulance finally came, I ran downstairs to my aunt's side. She quickly told me to not look as she held me next to her side. People that had never given me a second glance were holding onto my body, saying not to look and how brave of a child I was. Why was I brave? My daddy just hadn't woken up and for some reason, the ambulance was here. I didn't do anything at all. My aunt had to leave me, leaving me in the arms of my great grandmother, and she hopped in the ambulance with my daddy. I didn't see them for a while after that. Instead, my great grandmother took me into her car and took us back to what felt like the most loving house someone could ever hope to be in.

Today was supposed to be special. My mommy was coming to my Halloween parade with the momom I was torn away from and my other aunt. I was going to see her and wave to her in my costume and then get to hug her. Why did it have to get ruined? I remember my little brain telling myself that today was my turn to have something bad happen. Today, I had deserved it. Everyone has something bad happen to them and it was just a part of life. It was only fair.

What kind of fucked up thinking is that for a child? Thinking in a way that only an adult should be thinking.

A lot of things changed that day. I became (more of) a grown-up that day. My childhood was ruined that day. I learned how fucking horrible drugs were on that day.

My father woke up. I remember going to the hospital and somehow, all of my family was there. All my aunts, uncles, and cousins were there. Some came from Manalapan and some came from deep in

New York. Every single person was there, waiting for the news. My grandmother was speaking to the receptionist, crying her beautiful eyes out. My Aunt Karen and Uncle Jeffrey were telling me about a dog they were going to adopt to take my mind off of everything. I loved dogs but it only numbed the situation a little.

On October 31st, 2002, my father had a drug overdose. I was eight years old when I found him naked in his own throw up. My great grandmother, god bless her soul, tried telling everyone it was because he took too much of his medicine because his back hurt and he was just really sleepy. Families do not come together with tears running down their faces from someone being sleepy, but it eased my mind. It eased my mind until that night and many nights after that. I don't think anyone realized how badly that would fuck me up.

Imagine This:

You are no older than eight years old. It's a cold night, with winds harsh enough to knock your perfect bowl cut of a hairdo around. Your father has picked you up from the safe confines of your grandmother's house, the only place that no harm has touched you. In your tiny head, you thought the plan was to go to your other grandparents' house in Staten Island, some 45 minutes away. Your father is nodding off at the wheel, and you think he's just tired, so you try to put the music loud to wake him up. You understand, sometimes Momom has to be really loud to get you up for school, after all! It happens. He gets annoyed, muttering under cigarette-tinted breaths to knock it off. You don't know where you are, the graffiti landmarks don't match the ones that lead you to New York. You are scared. You don't know why, but you are scared and the hero of your life, known as your father, is not enough to calm these nerves, but you ignore it. He will protect you. He will not put you in harm's way.

You pull into a foreign parking lot. You don't really know what it is, but it kinda looks like the place Daddy takes his cars that never seem to work to get fixed. You sense the weight of the world coming off your dad's shoulders as he smiles at you. You love him, he is your world since Mommy is gone because she's sick. He tells you that you're allowed to come in with him, but there's no point since he'll be right back. You tell him that's fine! You'll even protect the car for him, since you know it's his favorite one he's had! He smiles and leaves.

Hour one passes. Now you're getting bored. You aren't allowed to use your Gameboy Color on the weekends you spend with him. You can see how cold it is outside by the way the trees viciously threaten to uproot from their spots on the ground and you kind of wish he let you keep the car on, but it's okay. The heat still kind of remains, and he'll be back any minute. It's no big deal. The light shut off in the main lobby of the building. It's no big deal.

It is now hour three. You are scared. What happened to Daddy? Did he forget about you? Did someone hurt him? You have no phone. You've been crying and you know no one can hear you, so you try to honk the horn. It doesn't help and now panic sets in. How far are either Momom's house? You heard stories about bad people taking little girls like you, and you are scared to get out of the car. Daddy doesn't let you use the phone anyway, you're not allowed to answer it. You are so scared. You have to pee, and you don't want to be made fun of for peeing your pants. Somehow, deep within your tiny body, you get the courage to get out of the gray Jeep Chrysler and go inside that building. You want to go home with your Daddy now, and you'll do it yourself. You pull your purple bubble coat with the faux fur trim around you tighter and slowly make your way to the door. Your chubby hands tremble as you reach for the door handle, and yet somehow you still manage to pull. You yank with all your strength, and that god damned door doesn't open. You start crying again.

It has now been four hours and thirty minutes. You can't breathe. The cold has reached inside the vehicle, and you are now scared. You have convinced yourself this is it: you will be left here. You cry out for your grandmothers and your mother. You miss your absent Mommy more than anything in the world. When was the last time you saw her? Did you tell Momom you loved her before you left? What about your dog, Kiara, the one you've had since you were four years old? You cry, and that is all you can do.

Finally, your father came back, lightly joking how you should've came in because it was so fun. There was carnival style popcorn! There was a dog that was friendly! It was so nice in there, and you had no reason to stay out here! The circles under his eyes disappeared, and the fun daddy was back. You were so happy you forgot all about what happened. You didn't realize how much this moment would really mess your whole head up. You didn't realize that when you were going to get drugs yourself, that your PTSD would kick in and you would feel like you were the little girl again. You didn't realize you would cry about this night a lot.

As a child, I was often bouncing from state to state, sleeping in whichever house felt the safest at that time to my parents. I was an innocent child, not asking for much besides love and care, and getting only the opposite as my parents chose to be strung out on heroin. I'm sure you've seen on news outlets, and from Facebook posters alike, the overwhelming amount of parents being recorded nodding out with their children crying in the backseat, a diaper full of pee and an empty stomach. That was me. Maybe besides the food part, as I was always a chubby little girl, but that was me. Crying to my grandparents and begging them to bring my parents home, staying up hours of the night sitting on the stairs, waiting for them to walk through the doors; that was me.

As previously stated I moved a lot. By the time I was in 10th grade (I was held back one year) I was in my 8th school. My 8th! Most kids went to elementary, middle, high school that was planned for them since they were in the womb and here I was, on my 8th. It was an alternative night school, which I didn't realize would take such a fucking toll on my life.

My childhood, however, was what nightmares are made of. Never knowing when your mother would walk in the door, hearing the whispers and arguments of grandparents about other caretakers being on drugs, and never knowing when something bad would, inevitably, happen again.

I classify my childhood into two sections: White Oak Lane and Tynan Road (or was it street? I blocked most of those memories out.) White Oak Lane was where my father had his overdose stunt. We lived in a small apartment that was connected to our landlord, who proved to only be decent during the overdose and when I wanted to swim in their pool. I cannot tell you how much I hated that apartment, and if you walked into the door that lead to the beige carpeted one bedroom space you'd learn to despise it as well. I don't know if it was because of all the times I cried, or maybe it was all the times I would sit locked in the living room, but the feeling of dread hit you like a prized boxer on his best day. More days than none my father had strange people coming in and out of the apartment, locking themselves in his room for what felt like an eternity for a child, but may have been an hour. Wednesday night was shower night. I was taking two a week and my father used to sit me on his lap and comb my hair out, but after awhile it slowly dimmed down to only once a night. Dinner was either Hawaiian pizza from dominos, quesadillas from the Colonnade Diner, or ham and honey mustard sandwiches from the George Foreman grille - those were my favorite. I remember having to get ketchup out of the drawer that was filled with pills. Pills and fucking ketchup.

I never knew one person for too long. My father's best friend was Damien, who I think of now as making my skin crawl. There was Kelly, too - I think they still talk. Those were the only people I knew on a first name basis, besides that people were just faces. The fat guy and his blonde girlfriend, the dark haired girl that was supposedly daddy's girlfriend that I only saw once. Nobody ever stayed, and I to this day I feel like someone had to know what was going on. I was sworn to secrecy, yes - but how well could an eight year old be at that? Why the fuck did nobody bother to save me from that apartment?

Tynan was worse in different ways. My mother worked her fucking ass off for the rent while my father spent it all to get high. I remember how mad she was when one of my dad's drug buddies knocked on the door looking for him and refused to believe us, and how scared I was when a man knocked on the door and for some reason thought I was head of household and gave us our eviction letter. My mother had her suspicions that my dad was spending her money on drugs and this just proved it. My dad went to rehab twice in that apartment, both times me being told he was sick just like when he wouldn't wake up. The first time because 'the place was like a snake pit' he screamed over the phone (and I thought there was an actual pit of snakes, and was extremely upset with my family for sending him there.) The second time was more emotional as he truly tried, I believe. He gave us matching bracelets and told me every night at 9 P.M to think of him and he would think of me, and I cannot tell you how hard I cried every night at 9. My parents got into a lot of fist fights, some including pots and pans. I remember listening to my Good Charlotte CD and 'My Bloody Valentine' came on - I thought the thunder and lightning and screaming were only part of the track until I took my headphones off. I think about that night a lot; I think about how the sounds of pots and pans being dropped still makes my heart stop in its place.

Drugs were always a part of my life, I think. I don't remember the exact age, I just remember one day my mother no longer being around me. No longer were warm hugs and a person to kiss away the pains of scrapes and bruises, in place were night terrors. I had two dreams that would come and go as they please. The first was simple: We were always at a CVS, my mother and I. I would wait in the car and she'd run in, telling me she'd be back in a moment. She never came. Instead people came up to the car and laughed at me, telling me how silly I was for believing she'd be back.

The second stung my chest a little bit more whenever I thought about it. I would be at a store with my 'fake' mommy, and run into a different aisle to look at a toy and there was a woman. She'd turn around and look at me, and as soon as I recognized her to be my true mother, she'd laugh and say I was nuts, going back to a cart that had a baby that had a striking resemblance to me.

The gist of my dreams were always simple: mommy was going somewhere and she'd disappear, or I would see her in public and either I wouldn't recognize her, or she wouldn't recognize me. It tore me up inside. I'd wake up crying, never able to sleep in my own bed until I was 10 years old out of fear whoever was taking care of me would leave. I would have to touch their face to go to sleep, and I still have to now (thank god my husband doesn't think I'm a creep.) I was always bribed to sleep in my own room, my grandparents in Staten Island tried to give me the world while my grandparents in Trenton were a little more okay with it. They asked if I had a pretty room would I sleep in it, and gave me a 'princess' room to try. The pink walls and canopy bed didn't do shit besides give me a place to cry while holding all the letters and gifts my mom would send through the mail.

My other go to place was the stairs. It gave me the perfect view of the front door that led to the busy suburban street of Bloomingdale Road. Every night I'd stay up a little later than I should, crying and begging someone, anyone, to bring my mommy home. No one listened, though, and I was by myself for awhile until someone had to wake me up and bring me to their room.

I remember seeing no bad in my mother until I we moved into our own apartment when I was 15. My mother always took my side, always hugging me and loving me more than I could ever ask for. She fought with the schools that gave me problems, trying her god damned best to make positive changes for me. She was always a beautiful person with these big green-blue eyes that to this day never stay one color when I look at her, they always radiated kindness; she always had a feel that you could talk to her, a feature that even my closest friends took advantage of. A lot of things changed when I was 15, I thought I was an adult and often challenged my mother and she took none of my shit. We fought a lot, and she was a nasty person when I made her be. Before I understood methadone, I would constantly yell at her. I felt as if she was sleeping her life away, not taking life by the horns like I thought I was.

When I started getting high, I saw a lot worse in her. She knew I'd be dope sick on the couch and throw me 20$ for myself, then give me a 160$ and make me walk the half-hour to get her Adderall or Molly. One time she cursed me out and threw me out of the house until I could get her any upper, so I left the house while sobbing and hiccupping into my grandmother's car. She wanted me to go to my best friend at the times house and steal all his Adderall - she was mad I wasn't with him and threatened me again when she found out I was actually with my momom. She wouldn't let me get off the phone, she wanted to tear my forces down and break me apart and to this day I don't know why. I brought her home a pill bottle full of Klonopin to maybe help her - she thought I was patronizing her. She threw them at me and made me lock myself in my room. The only time I ever cried that hard was when I was broke and sick.

My father is my twin. We have the same exact face, down to the hazel eyes that turn green when we tan. We have the same anger issues; the same 'I don't give a fuck' attitude. For all the shit I've talked about him in my life, for all the times I said he was a piece of shit, I see the good in him now. I see that he did try, and was just completely powerless to his addiction. I don't hold resentment towards him, and maybe if he was in New Jersey still instead of Florida it would be different, but for some crazy ass reason I just don't hate him. I remember always being scared of him as a child though and believing every word he said. One time when I was 8 he got too high and had to sleep on the couch, then woke me up in the morning to get his nose spray out of the car. I put my shoes on only to be met with them being filled with puke. Now I understand that he threw up from being too fucked up, but back then I believed that his tummy hurt.

He wasn't ever fully around. He'd show up every other weekend and take me to my grandmother's (his mother's) house in Staten Island and stay in the basement - whenever I walked downstairs the floor was filthy with dutch guts and bad liquor. We didn't ever really talk, either. I remember my step dad asking what he and I did, what we talked about and didn't believe me when I said nothing. My mother had to explain that was normal, and my step dad just couldn't understand. He came when there was money. My 15th birthday he called (two days late) and then asked what I got - when I told him how much he asked for 30$ - then upped it to 60$. He never paid me back, and I only had 10$ to myself left.

I was around eight or nine years old when my mother came back into my life, 10 when she had enough fist fights with my father and moved her and me back to Hamilton, New Jersey with her father.

For a while everything was nice, and then I started 4th grade. I was literally tormented by these fucking school kids. I was different. I had a lisp, I was chubby, and I was as goth as a 10 year old could be (aka listen to Good Charlotte/From First To Last and wear Tripp pants) and those kids loved to make fun of me for it.

My phone was off the hook with pre-pubescent boys telling me to kill myself, I wasn't allowed on my online instant messenger (AIM) past a certain time because the spam messages just kept coming. Rocks were always being pegged at my window, and more than enough times I had to throw my food out because they would call me fat and the teacher would let it happen, sometimes laughing with them.

Middle school was a tiny bit kinder as I ditched the Tripp pants for black skinny jeans and band t-shirts. I was kind of popular until everyone I was friends with became friends with my old bullies, after that I was a social outcast until 8th grade. 7th grade was a bad year, I learned about cutting myself and what it was like to truly fight with my mother. Gone were the days I'd sleep next to her and tell her I love her, replacing them were nights of me yelling that I wish she never came back into my life and blasting whatever god awful screamo music I could find. She found a new boyfriend, Mike, who for some reason I couldn't stand. He did his fair share of awful shit, like trying to be a father while I didn't have a good (or at sometimes, any) relationship with my own, telling my mother to not let me go to the hospital when I had bronchitis, or telling me to grow up. For a 13 year old growing through personal changes, that was damn rude.

Then one day, they brought me to a therapist who assessed my mind like no other. I told her about the night terrors I had daily, and how sometimes I felt like I was 8 years old again and had to wake my daddy up but he just wouldn't - she introduced me to PTSD. I told her how when I was in crowds I would have to run away and find somewhere quiet and lonesome because I got jittery and scared and my heart would beat out of my chest - she introduced me to panic attacks. I told her how I would sleep to pass the days, and how I found myself crying and yelling for no reason - she introduced me to depression. I told her this, I told her that; I told her everything that my mind was doing, and it turned out I had depersonalization disorder, along with some PTSD and depression. I was 12 years old and on Klonopin, Zoloft, Geodon, Abilify, and Trazodone. I hated how when I didn't take one thing my body felt like it was literally being zapped - like I was being electrocuted by high volts. I stopped cold turkey when I went to my grandparents in Staten Island one weekend to visit them and my father and noticed almost all of my Klonopin was gone.

8th grade was different. I was confident. I knew I was pretty, I knew I was skinny, and I knew I was funny. I didn't give a fuck about anyone that tried to bully me because I discovered fighting and it was so COOL to punch people in the face. It was cool to fight people and watch them be bloody and tear stained and have their friends too afraid to talk shit. I loved every second of it.

I got drunk for the first time that year. I went to a wedding with my father and his side of the family, his mission to "get me drunk at my first wedding." It started with a grey goose and orange juice, then champagne, then after the wedding I did my first shot at the ice bar and remember how amazing I feel when my father and cousin said I did it perfectly. I felt like after so many wrong trials in my life, after always feeling like I was doing something wrong, I finally did something right and impressed my father. That's all I ever wanted.

I smoked cigarettes for the first time, too. I was always friends with older kids, and my best friend in the whole world, Taylor introduced me to them. I hung onto her every word, her every move; obviously I had to do what she was doing or I wouldn't be cool. Besides, I was in 7th/8th grade and she was in 9th/10th, I had to be kinda cool or she wouldn't even be hanging out with me, right?

9th grade, however, is when everything changed. No longer was I a confident 14 year old, no. Instead, I was replaced by a shy, naive child who would do anything to fit in. Older kids inviting me, of all people to skip class to go to Sev (7-11)?! Obviously, I'm doing it.

My mother and I got an apartment by ourselves in Trenton, New Jersey. Although only about 10 minutes away from the house I was in at the time, the area was much worse, much tougher. Drug dealers flooded the streets, prostitutes sat outside porches attached to row homes, and my own apartment was even falling apart when we began to rent it. That's all we could afford, though, and my Popop wanted us out ASAP. Gone were the days that we had so much food we were allowed to be picky, replacing them were now days where all we had was 75$ on a food stamp card to last us a month. We would have the condiments for a sandwich, but not the food. We had enough white rice to last years, and if we were lucky we'd spend our change on snacks at the Dollar General to hold us over. I resented my Popop so badly for making us move away from our comfy home in the suburbs. No one deserved to move to this hell. I got in a lot more trouble. I started skipping schools and getting drunk on cheap alcohol and dated boys with 7-page police records.

And then one day I had to go to the vice principal's office because I got in trouble for skipping my algebra class. There he was in his 5'4, lazy eyed glory: the boy who'd change my little world.

Chapter Two

For reasons I'm not getting into, I would rather not write about this person for more than I should, however, they play an important role as much as I wish they hadn't. This was my first true relationship. I was 14, I lost my virginity and thought I was in love. I hung onto every last word of his. He would tell me to steal, I'd steal. He would tell me to graffiti the broken down buildings that resided our neighborhoods and I would do it, all the while holding cheap cans of spray paint in my oversized purse. He would tell me to fight and I would do it, even if it was with his family. I was never home, instead I got drunk off of Olde English and listened to bands like Brand New and even French Montana when he first came out, thinking this is what life was supposed to be like. I thought I was supposed to cry most nights; I thought it was normal for boyfriends to call you 'fat' or even 'kyke' or even try to tear your relationship with your family up. I thought it was fucking normal, and maybe it was because of the way my mother was treated by the men in her life, I don't know. But I was living and breathing in mental abuse for two years and thought it was okay. His name was David.

When I was 16, I got switched to the alternative night school that occupied one of the high schools in my town. I met who I thought would be my best friend. Marie. She was beautiful, and had more experience in life than me and I envied her. I wanted to be her. We hung out every god damned day, residing in our friend's basement while he snorted blue's (aka Roxy 30's) that he crushed via hose grinder. None of us ever really fucked around - just the occasional 'bump' here and there, but that changed way too quickly for my liking. We'd drink and smoke bad weed here and there, but that was it. We opted for playing video games and giving our money to that same friend who promised things in return - i.e taking us to Seaside, going to the mall, paying us back. Obviously, it never happened.

One day, everything changed and I swear to God I felt it coming. I felt it in the wind that blew my hair around - I felt it when the trees waved me down. It was difficult to breathe and my head was screaming what was going on, but like any 16 year girl, I ignored it. I ignored it until I came back from Staten Island one weekend and a kid in our friend group told me my biggest fears had come true - my boyfriend and best friend were hooking up.

I can't really tell you what happened after I found out. I called my Aunt Erica screaming. I punched the wall at Quick Chek and made a hole I'd point at for years to come. I called my (ex) boyfriend's mother who screamed profanities and picked me up in the family's grey jeep - she bought me a 40 and hugged me while I cried and threw up, telling me I deserved a handsome doctor in Florida and not her son. Life kinda spiraled out of control after that but I still tried every single fucking day to convince him to leave her. I went to parties when only David was there, then got drunk when she showed up and cried when she would kiss him in front of me.

The pain of seeing your ex best friend and your now ex boyfriend hook up in front of you is something no one should *ever* fucking go through. I let my life spiral from there.

I hung out with whatever friend group I had, doing almost anything to avoid the ache in my chest. I started partying a lot but never EVER did a pill. I smoked bad weed and drank even worse alcohol, talking to guys but never going any further than that. For awhile, and it literally disrespects every cell in my being, I was even the side chick - that's when the roxy's came into play. David and his new girlfriend were snorting blues any chance they got until she got pregnant. She dipped for a little while around November and I moseyed my way in, hating every second of my pathetic life. I realize now that I only wanted to feel loved, and to this day feel sorry for ever butting in. I was lonely, and needed something to fill my lonely nights - and for awhile this made me stop crying. Shit was going up my nose and I was content, thinking I had my boyfriend back while that was the opposite.

I hated blues. Throughout the whole little side girl thing, I maybe did about 10 whole ones altogether. I always threw up and never got the high feeling - I never understood why everyone loved it. One time a bunch of us were hanging out in the Rite Aid parking lot and the cops showed up. I was already lying down in my friend's backseat because I felt puke coming, but he harshly whispered for me to sit up because the cops were coming to check him. As soon as I opened them I was met with a harsh flashlight - I obviously fucking yaked. I threw up right as one cop was checking the car and another was stepping in it.I threw up again in my apartment hallway, telling my mother I just drank too much.

In June of 2012 I had found a steady friend group - Scott, Jess, Nicky, Joey, Mike, Jessy, Brent - I literally surrounded myself with them at all times. I dropped out of High School and partied and drank like a fucking fish. I met Ecstasy for the first time and that was it. The rest was fucking history. Every other day we were going to Seaside, spending 60$ on cheap motels and 100$ on ten pills. Mario Stars, Rolex's, Simpsons, Ninja Turtles - you name it I swallowed it and never had a better time in my life. We ran up and down the shaky boardwalks with no care in the world - giving the finger and trying to fight anyone who stopped us. Do you remember that song, "Glad You Came"? That was our anthem, as corny as it sounded. It was my birthday weekend and Jess (my new and more loyal best friend) told the DJ it was my 21st (but really only my 17th) birthday and that he HAD to play it - he did, and included a nice "Happy 21st Kayla, keep rolling" message in there and I remember my heart pounding with excitement. I then promptly threw up on a lady who yelled, but I muttered a 'go fuck yourself' as I wiped my mouth off.

We had fun - I forgot all my problems. We went to the Canal at Washington's Crossing and went off rope swings. It was my first time and I, Kayla Small, scaredy cat of the world went off the highest one! It was great until my heart beat out of my chest and I remember hearing you could have a heart attack on ecstasy; it was great until my leg got caught in the rope and I was dangling upside down. My mother even gave me the okay! She even asked me to roll with her and I thought she was so fucking badass and so did all my friends.

And then one night, Nicky, Jess, and I went back to Seaside at around 3 in the morning and were drinking under the boardwalk when some random kid came up to us. John? I don't know, I forgot his fucking name. We talked to him for awhile and low and behold, he brought out a bag of dope. He asked if we had ever done any because if we did, he'd give us a bump. Jess quickly said yes, and I said yes right after her even though it was a bold face lie. I just wanted to fit in again, and in the back of my head, I remembered the rumors I heard about David doing dope. I did dope for the first time that day, under a boardwalk with three people splitting one five dollar bag. I got high for the first time off of heroin that day. I nodded out on the drive home that day, thinking it would never touch my hands again.

I wish I never went to Seaside that night.

Right: Just me, nothing fancy. Left: Jess, me, Brent. Four E pills deep.

Chapter Three

I forgot about that night in Seaside. I started dating someone new, Jordan. A little scrawny kid that had lied about his whole life up to a point and for some reason, it intrigued me. I had to know this dope head, lead singer of a band and a 'crazy good fighter'. He was in a 'band' (and I use that term very loosely) with my best friend Scott, and from there we had a little group. Jordan, Scott, Seth and a kid named Loko of all things. Thinking back, it was really fucking nerdy but I was on top of the world. I had friends, a 'cool' boyfriend; the ache in my chest at night went away, even if the childhood PTSD didn't.

Before I start this chapter head on, I wanna say one thing - Jordan would not sleepover my house without an opiate in hand, he stated. I could never find anything because all my connects had run out, so he never came over. And then, everything changed. Just that simple.

They came in an old Lincoln (I think it was a Lincoln, anyway. I'm not good with cars) - three of them pulled up to Scott's house. A man, his girlfriend, and her little sister. They had beautiful smiles with husky laughs that made you wanna know why they were laughing, you wanted to get in on the secret. They moved together, almost as if they had synchronized their movements and pre-planned this day years ago. I just wanted to know them. I wanted to know everything about them, what their favorite foods were and where they fucking shopped.

Jordan's eyes lit up. "We can get dope" he whispered harshly, and by the time I was nodding my head he was already next to the only boy in the group. After a few seconds they waved me over, and my legs felt like fucking jello as I walked down Scott's steps. "How much do you need? A bun is only 50..." He said quietly, his eyes peeking over his aviators. I stuttered my words, trying to sound cool but coming out like an idiot. "I mean, I probably one need t-t-three...three bags." You could tell he was annoyed by my words. "I mean, I can get you a whole bun for 50! You've probably been getting them for a lot more than that, and I would only need three out of ten.."

I don't know why I said yes. I don't know why I dug through my messy Chanel purse I found at *Red White And Blue*, but for some reason I did. I handed him 50 fucking dollars and they left, Jordan muttering something about how he'll be right back. For the 15 minutes that they were gone, I was on Erowid's Vault, reading everyone's story about the first time they did heroin as my first time was really just a sample. I was nervous. What if I die? What if I overdose and my mother finds me dead, her worst fears of her only child doing the same drug that destroyed her life becoming true?

"But who fucking cares" ran through my mind as I chain smoked newports on the porch. *"I'm finally apart of something."* I guess that's all I ever wanted in life - to be apart of something; to feel needed. I wanted to have a group of friends to take pictures with and I finally got that. I was young, I just turned 17 and I was allowed to fuck up. I wouldn't become addicted to dope - only losers do that. Only loser's become junkies. I'm popular, I'm funny, I'm cute. I have way too much shit going on.

I didn't realize how simple it was, how one mistake would change everything. To be honest, I completely forgot the bundle of heroin in my purse, black stamped *'La Cura'*. So when all of us drove down I-95 was Atilla blasting, going more than the legal limit, I wasn't worried. All of us came back to my apartment and hung outside in my oversized room, equipped with a twin size bed with pink and zebra print sheets. *Thank God I finally cleaned my room.* My mother was away for the weekend, not a single thought in her head that her only child was about to fuck up her life.

I remember Scott and Seth coming back from Quick Chek with meatball subs in hand while Loko and Jordan sat around, talking about different bands and vocals and what the fuck ever. I went in my purse to grab a cigarette pack and my hands brushed the glassine bags. I guess Jordan saw the look on my face when I touched it because his missing-brace infested mouth smiled large. It was kind of telepathic after that. *You wanna do the bags now, Kayla? Duh.*

He kicked everyone out, just like that with some excuse on how I was tired. I remember hugging my friends tightly, telling them to be careful with a shaking body. They had no idea I just bought a bundle of dope in front of them. My friend since David came over, John. He was telling me stories about how he had become a dope head and wanted to get high with me and my new boyfriend. He wanted to give the OK to 'date his older sis'. He really just wanted free drugs, I'm sure of now. Our friendship was tight, but nobody ever just denies free drugs.

I took out the bags and handed them over to my boyfriend who looked like a lost puppy in the rain. He literally inspected the bags, looking at every corner and tried to open them. I probably should've known he had never done dope at that point. I probably should've known him and John had never done dope by the way they took a fucking butter knife and tried to cut the bag open. For those unaware, in New Jersey, we have these little glassine bags that are some inches long, with three folds. The stamp is always at the bottom, and they come in a little square with a tiny piece of tape shutting them before you open it. Obviously, any experienced heroin user would know to just peel the tape off. I don't know why I was so naive. I don't know why I let this happen.

My life was lined up on the dresser I had since I moved to Jersey from Staten Island at that point. The whitish-brown tinted line was staring at my stupid face, while John and Jordan were watching me with anticipation. I don't know why I had to be the first one - but here I was. With a bic pen cut into a nice sized snorting straw in my nose, one shaky finger plugging the other one. I breathed in and...that was it. The powder went up my nose with such a ferocity that it took my breath away. It burned, and the taste, the drip...*oh god the drip.* It beat the drip blue's give me by a thousand.

I sat on the bed, my boyfriend in tow while John sat on the computer chair that was tossed in my room. We all had cigarettes lit, courtesy of John's' father who gave them to him before dropping him off. I caught up with John, asking about the old neighborhood and how various people were doing. I asked if he remembered the time I called him while rolling face and he laughed, then said "Damn sis, I missed you yo." I smiled back, remarking how I felt so fucking comfortable.

It may have been ten minutes, I don't know. I remember thinking every twitch or itch in my body was because of the opiate, until those ten minutes passed. I remember picking another cigarette up, lighting it, and then blinking, then when I opened my eyes from the blink all that was left was cigarette ash on black yoga pants. John laughed, and Jordan wiped the ash off of my pants.

That was it. That's all I really remember. After some time John left, saying we must have got bad dope because he wasn't nodding out but his step-brother called someone and someone got in touch with me, saying John nodded out the whole night. He even drooled on himself. I remember laughing and keeping a mental note of it, so anytime John asked for more because of his 'high tolerance' I brought that night up. August 17th, 2012 - the first time I truly did heroin. I brought up August 17th.

Scott never found out about that secretive drug deal, either. He never knew it all started in his driveway.

I remember that night before going to sleep, Jordan told me he loved me and I said thanks. Just 'thanks'. I didn't really know what else to say, honestly. I was still a tiny, eensy little bit getting over everything. Besides, 'love' had nothing I wanted. I didn't want to be lonely, yes - but I didn't want everything else that came with relationships. The trust issues, the crying, the complacency. I didn't want to feel that something that *may* of had the potential to fizzle and dry out. I didn't think I would be able to emotionally handle that again.

But we went to sleep, and I must have mustered out an 'I love you too', because the next morning that was the first thing he said to me.

It took us a little bit to wake up the next day, but we had already made plans to go to Oxford Valley Mall with the group. We got ready, and this time it was me to say, "do you wanna do some bags?" Obviously, we did and off we went, not letting anybody catch onto us. Going to the mall, I was fine. I wasn't as high as last night, but I kept telling myself I was so I might feel something (a 'trick' I learned from the ecstasy days.) It was the ride going to someone's house that I felt weird. I remember leaning my head inside the right side passenger door, the rough material almost scratching my face. I had the window down and tried my best not to throw up, simultaneously holding back tears because this just HAD to be what dying felt like. I wasn't warm and fuzzy like last night or kind of even this morning, instead I was hot and had cold sweats forming everywhere they could, while I had to push Jordan off me while he was trying to ask if I was okay. I don't know what happened, and to this day I still don't. I know I probably just had to throw up because of the diesel, but I don't know why I felt like I was dying. I never felt like that ever again even, when I had to throw up.

I missed Jess. She was my best friend and I had been neglecting her calls when I switched friend groups. I knew what I was doing was wrong - people just don't look at people who do dope kindly. If anybody found out, my reputation was over. I had 2 bags left - Jordan and I would finish them and that would be it - no harm done. No one would have to know and he'd get over his ridiculous fear of sleeping over a girl's house or whatever he had. This wasn't a life I was supposed to live and I knew it. I was going to do a 360...as long as I didn't die in the back of this messy ass Honda civic.

I don't really remember where we went after my 'almost-dying' either. I think we went to this kid Josh's house who lived in Croydon. I do remember, however, feeling better and feeling happy again. Once more, I had completely forgotten about the dope in my purse. We were all joking around, running around the streets and bouncing off cars. I remember us laughing at Seth when he tried to hit on my friend Angie, or this random kid's face when I cockily said I'd go tagging with him...and my shit would like better than his. I can't express the feelings I had through these pages, no matter the words I type out. As I'm writing this it's 8:00 P.M. and I'm at work - almost in tears as I remember how fucking fun 2012 was. I had experiences I will never again go through, drug induced or not. I met a million and one fucking people running around different states and cities, all with a smile on my face. I never realized I would miss those days. I never realized how fucking quickly they would disappear from me.

Scott had dropped me and Jordan at his house. I took a shower and put my hair up in a towel when I shyly reminded him we had two more bags. Then, for some crazy reason, a look came upon his face...pain? Sadness? No. He was obviously acting as he muttered out "Okay, but we're never doing this again." He was obviously again acting when between cutting up the lines with my photo ID he said "I'm serious, Kayla. We're not going to be like those people we talk about." Maybe he had meant it. I'm pretty sure I knew I was making empty promises, but I was so nervous that I was over his house that I just wanted to put something up my nose. Again, I don't remember much besides going to sleep without being shaky and having no night terrors.

The next day I did dope, too. It was the first time I went to cop. The strangers from a few days ago (we made 7 bags last 2 or 3 days) picked us up from my apartment on Hamilton Ave and took us to around the corner, maybe some 5 minutes away by Greenwood. I remember sitting so fucking still, barely even laughing when someone made a joke. I kept my eyes to the carpeted ground, not wanting to make eye contact. I don't know why. I don't know if it was because I was just being a huge wimp, or because I didn't want these people to think I was taking their dealer or what, but I kept my eyes to the ground besides when he showed up to the car. He had a hearty laugh but quickly muttered out that we were being sketch and ran off. I don't remember the stamp, but I remember smiling when I saw it was red. Beat It, maybe? I don't know. All that mattered was that it was red and anyone I knew that did dope bragged about red stamps and look what I got.

We went to a bonfire right after that, like literally right after. Scott was actually waiting in his car out front of my apartment. I remember the way I ran off my porch and jumped off the stairs was like I was dancing. The night time summer breeze hit my skin like kiss after kiss, as if wanting me to be in the most amazing state of euphoria I could be in. I got in the front seat and buckled my seat belt, rolling the windows down and putting my tanned legs up. John was already in the backseat, automatically jealous as Jordan told him about the stamp we got. I smiled, looking back and saying how fucking good it was. Scott made some stupid joke and I laughed a real fucking laugh - not my fake "hmph" noise. I felt light on my feet. You know when you're on hardwood floors and you have socks in, and you kinda just glide about? I felt like that, except I was walking on grass or tar filled streets and had flip-flops on.

I remember going to Angie's bonfire and it being filled with strangers. Pretty faces I've seen on Facebook and Instagram but never in person but I was fine. I wasn't a nervous wreck and wasn't worried, no. I was confident. If they asked me questions they addressed me by name, they knew who I was. I remember leaning my head back on the chair, my long black hair falling over the chair like a straight perfect waterfall and someone actually complimented it, with no snark! What is going on?

The next couple of days and even weeks kept going like that. We'd get a bun, split it evenly and make it last for a few days, and that was it. I even reunited with my friend with the basement one night when he took me to cop. He took us at like midnight to an Extended Stay and I remember the dude sitting passenger seat with him chopped up his line and held it out for him as he snorted it, driving down rt 1. I was sad, though. He had moved from blues to actual dope now, and since he always had a constant supply of money his habit was bad. He ended up going to rehab a few short weeks later and is still clean last time I checked.

Around September, a mutual friend had a huge end of summer pool party and the whole group went. Scott, Jordan, Seth, Loko, John - even the strangers from the first time I did drugs. Brian, Christina, Taylor - they came and it was the first time I actually talked to them. Brian was quiet, harder to get into and it made me nervous. I didn't want to seem annoying like I was always so used to so I usually stayed away from him, casually talking to Christina and her little sister Taylor here and there. We shared jokes about her cool lighter that was also a cigarette holder, and how silly all the scene kids at the pool party looked. After a while, Brian and Jordan played their acoustic set (they were in a little band and John put their songs on a CD, calling it a demo) and we all sang along as best as we could. I was proud that I knew my boyfriend's lyrics, and was actually singing them! I wasn't getting nervous and didn't clam up until all the sudden my throat started to hurt and I started to sweat. Loko, a lot bigger than me, was sitting on my lap and I didn't care up until that point. I pushed him off, saying sorry my body was just killing me and tried to walk it off. At this point, I had only been using about every day for a month. I didn't think it could be withdrawal, I thought I just got my regular sinus infection my deviated septum loved to give me. But at the same time, I felt like I was fucking dying while I was sitting in a chair by myself as my friends were splashing in the pool. John came up to me for a second, asking if I was okay. "I'm really, really sick" I croaked out, wiping sweat off my forehead. "Did you do dope today?"

Did I do dope today? No. David came to my apartment though, sister and newborn child whose mother was Marie in tow. I held her beautiful little body for awhile, and I didn't feel sick then - I actually felt relieved. Relieved she was so beautiful, relieved she came out perfect and resembling his mother who had died 6 months or so prior. I moved around my apartment quickly as he and my current boyfriend talked about different stamps, as Scott was kind of just in my room not knowing what to do - just wanting to leave and take us all to the pool party. I wasn't sick then, and he was probably just asking if I had bags for him. "No," I answered, coughing out mucus. "Well, there you go." He quickly said. "I think you're dope sick." I scoffed, brushing it off as him just being way over dramatic again and shooed him away, thinking in my head that if this is dope sick I'll stop today. Today never came.

One night a few weeks after, Scott took us to a party one night at the Red Roof Inn, Brent was hosting it and I was excited to meet up with my old group. Scott had slowly stopped hanging out with us, something he often did with friend groups and I bit my tongue in his presence. I checked the tiny mirror that was lodged inside the overhead, making sure a thousand times that I didn't look like a 'junkie'. I don't even think I did dope that night, I think I only had like 10$ to my name. I wasn't as excited to drink as I would have been pre-dope, and I remember getting easily annoyed at Scott trying to invite people I wanted nothing to do with.

We finally went up stairs after sitting in the car for what felt like an hour and I sat on the cheap material they call bedding, twisting off the top of a Bud Light Platinum and making small talk with everyone. Even though I was annoyed with every tiny thing, I was happy to see my old group. They were all there, faces all the same, same jokes and laughs. Jordan was playing a stupid beer game, talking to some random about weed when I heard Brent said Jess was coming.

Jess? Like, as if my best friend in the entire world Jess? I was so excited. "I'll text her to hurry up," I said quickly, pulling out my phone and making my fingers move a thousand miles a minute. She replied back that she'd be there in a half hour, she just got off work at this haunted farm and Brett just got her. I waited at that hotel room door like a fucking puppy, getting more and more angry with every person that walked in. I was annoyed, kinda drunk, and not engaging in any fun conversation. Jordan was annoying me more and more with every second, and I just wanted to leave.

And then she came in, like a fucking angel in scary clown makeup. She and Brett came in, sniffing a lot and I guess the look on her face set her off because she hugged me and brought me into the bathroom, muttering "I gotta talk to you about something."

We sat in the bathroom, I took a seat on the toilet as I quickly replied: "I already know, bitch."

She smiled, and as she took out a bag of dope we both laughed and word for word said: "I'm doing dope."

She started cracking up, then hit Brett lightly in the stomach. "See? Yo, I told you on the way here if there's anyone I'm tellin' it's Kayla. That's why you're my bitch, forreal."
I don't even think I had a chance to tell her I didn't do any today, because she already opened a bag and gave it to me, then split

another one with me. We talked about various stamps we had did like Casino Life, Taliban (which we agreed was our fucking favorite), and the first one I had ever did La Cura. We talked about when we had both started, agreeing sometime after that night in Seaside, and both gave each other stern looks when we talked about the dangers of shooting, and how never to do it. I was a lot calmer then, sniffing my nose here and there before we decided to leave the bathroom and keep this our little secret. I didn't notice how I thought everything was perfect after that. My boyfriend wasn't annoying me with how he ran around everywhere, and I forgot how the night before (and many, many nights before that) he faked a seizure from the dope. I forgot how upset I was with Scott, and I forgot my dumb ass, pessimistic mood. I was okay.

I drank and drank and drank, just how me and Jess and everyone in this hotel room had just two months prior. I made conversation and took pictures, some still on my Facebook page to this day. Someone I had been best friends with before I had even touched ecstasy, Megan, came over and I gave her the biggest hug I possibly could. Things made me happy again, my body was warm and I just wanted everyone around me to be as happy as I was.

Jess and I that night. October 9th, 2012.

A few hours later I was getting bored again, and Jess and I got on the subject about dealers. She said that hers didn't have a minimum, and I got overly excited.

"I have 10$ and would really, REALLY like a bag…" I said quietly, immediately embarrassed with how little money I had. She shrugged, going to the outside balcony to ask Brett. I got the same panic feeling I had as a kid when I had to ask my mom or dad a really important question and was scared of the outcome. To this day, I'm still like that unless I get in one of my not-so-rare anger moods. I start sweating and shaking and it literally takes every ounce of power in me to throw up the words. I don't remember how she told me we're down, we just need to wait to Brett to sober up but I was so fucking relieved. Then, like fucking Junkie Jesus himself blessing me, somehow word spread about the cops coming. I was only 17, so I grabbed my boyfriend who was playing some weird beer game (the one where you had to put a card on your forehead? I don't know) and followed Jess and Brett to his car. By the time I was in the backseat, I barely had time to shut the door - he was already on the move. Jordan asked what was going on, and I told him we were going to cop and that we heard the cops were on the way. I'm not too sure if I believed it or just needed an excuse to leave and get dope, but he didn't believe it. In fact, he was pissed. He thought we should save the money but Jess took the lead of the conversation and told him to shut up - it was my money and I could do what I wanted. He shut up.

We caught up even more at that point, talking about family and shit and getting along just how we used to. It didn't take long to get to the spot she was going to cop at, so when we parked out front of a laundromat on South Broad St. I asked how long it took for her guy to come. It wasn't a good area for four white people who more certainly than not look like junkies, and I remember my mother telling me horror stories about her days using on South Broad.

"We gotta leave you here," she said, taking the money I had in my palm. "He gets sketched out and there isn't even any room in the backseat."

The latter was true, but would I just leave her here with my money? I know she would never in a million years just rob me and leave me here to just sit and rot, but what if something happened? Or what if her addiction was worse than she had led on to and she would rob me? I guess she saw the panic in both mine and Jordan's eyes because she quickly assured us she'd be right back. "My dude is really quick and you know I would never in a million years do anything to fuck you over like that. Come on, Kayla."

I didn't say anything, just nodded back as I hiked my purse strap around my shoulder and left the vehicle and entered the cold, late September early October New Jersey weather. "I"ll be right back!" Jess shouted from the passenger side window as Brett made a left onto one of the side streets. When they were out of view I turned to my boyfriend who was already sitting on the steps, his tiny body shivering in the cold. Some parts of life hit me in the face then. Who the fuck was I? Was I really doing this to myself right now? I was only 17 years old, and just barely at that. How did I let control of my life go so fast?

I thought about the time I was only a teenager and sleeping on the top bunk, my mom on the bottom because we had to share a room when we escaped New York. She told me about the dangers of drugs and how each one felt, and when she got to heroin and described it as "being always warm and sleepy", I remember thinking that maybe I'd try that. I thought about when I was 14 my best friend, Ryan Wagner had died. He was so young and overdosed and when I called my mother crying she bawled back, asking if I was on heroin. I was so fucking mad that I shouted back no, hung up, then proceeded to cry again. I promised him on his casket to live for him and now here I was, across the street from a stop sign he tagged "Xani" one time he went to cop. I thought about David, and how he and Marie invited me to their new apartment a week or two before I ever got high. They did a bag right in front of me and Scott (who didn't know what it was, bless his soul) and then hung out with us on the two couches they pushed together in their broken down one bedroom apartment. David nodded out holding his month old child, making Marie get nuts and making Scott and I leave. I remember not crying and wondering if I was finally over the sting in my chest. I thought about my dad overdosing, and when was the last time I had a PTSD episode? It was so long ago now.

I looked to my boyfriend who's eyes were already on me. "It's only been five minutes, it's okay." I tried calming him down as best as I could, but he was a nervous wreck and I was no different. "We can't be here! This is a horrible place, Kayla. What the fuck is wrong with them?" He shouted, making me wince and then get angry.

"Jess wouldn't leave me stranded, no matter what." I wanted to end the conversation. Who was he to act like they wouldn't come back? They didn't even know each other besides tonight. She was *my* best friend, *I* knew her better than most. I knew she would come back, even if we had to sit here for what seemed like an hour. She wouldn't fuck us over, especially not over ten dollars. A few moments later we heard their car coming down Broad St, and there she was like an angel again. We got in the car and I pulled my wallet and straw out, happily taking the two bags from her.

"My bad for the wait, but I told you I'd be back. You know I wouldn't fuck you over like that."

I barely had time to tell her it was cool between chopping up lines and making sure my wallet was still during every speed bump. As fast as the dope went up my nose was as fast as I stopped caring. They dropped her off and I kissed her goodbye, telling her we'd chill ASAP.

It was hard for me to fall asleep that night, and not just because Jordan had faked another seizure. I was so disappointed in myself for having got this far into doing heroin. Maybe it was because I had never really had to wait anywhere out of my comfort zone for too long, or maybe it was because I was in the 'honeymoon stage' of me getting high, but now reality was very much real. I was slowly losing control of my life and thought I was still holding on to the reigns. It - dope - had me. It had me by the fucking veins and I couldn't lose its grip. I didn't want to stop. I could finally sleep at night, I was finally as confident as I should be. I could stop at any time, right? I was

mentally strong, I could do this. Drug addiction was for the weak, and I was unstoppable, right? No. I wasn't.

Chapter Four

I was no longer copping from Brian and Christina's dude all the time. Instead, Jordan had a friend we copped from one time who served as a middle man. His name was Max and I had known him from around the time I started the alternative night school and one of the people in my friend groups fought him. His Nana gave him a ride to my apartment and he called up some white kid from Hamilton who was getting high and selling bags for 7$ instead of 5$ to make a 20$ profit. But I had money because I wasn't fully into my addiction and told him to call him for me. A few minutes later Max came back with a horrible look on his face. "I only got seven…"

That was the first time I truly ever got mad from a drug deal. Between me yelling he had told me there was a kid in his car I was kinda friends with and I called him literally flipping shit. In between me yelling and threatening his life and reassured me he'd get the bags for me. I remember feeling so unstoppable after that, and after Max told my boyfriend that I was cool as shit. This day was the first time I ever got doubled sealed bags (they're kind of like the regular glassine bags, but inside little dime bag looking things and they're usually blue. These are usually an addict's favorite.) I don't remember how many I had given to Max or how many I had split between Jordan and me, but the next thing I knew I was on Max's bed throwing up literally every five minutes. When I wasn't throwing up I was nodding out with saltines he had given me to feel better or burning my arms with cigarettes on accident. The kid I had called earlier showed up at Max's house with my other three bags, apologizing. I hugged him and said it was no problem and that it was good to see him, and before I left he looked me in the eye and with the most sincerity I'd heard in the longest time said "Please, please tell me you're not doing this shit, Kayla. You're too fucking good for this." I smiled, hugging him once more and promising it wasn't me. I stumbled back to the house and threw up in Max's bushes, laying on the steps before his Nana took us home.

I was also copping most of the time from Jess, too. She got buns for 40$ and that left me with more money to spend on fast food than it did if we went through Brian. She also didn't ask for as many bags as he did, either and if she did it was only two. I also just liked being around her more because I was more comfortable. I knew I didn't have shit to worry about where as with Brian and Christina and her little sister, I felt I had to protect myself from them more. Of course, after a while, that changed, but this was before most things happened.

Jess would pick me up anytime Jordan went missing (he'd go to his house where he had no phone or wifi for his text messaging app, therefore I wouldn't talk to him for days at a time.) One time she wanted to visit this girl Jen, someone she had met when she was at Trenton Psych and introduced me to when I was drunk and went to visiting hours with her. Jen was finally at a halfway house kind of thing in south Jersey and the plan was to go to the mall, but only after we found money to get dope. Again, some mysterious ass force came thru for us because out of nowhere, a day early, Jess got her check from the haunted farm. Her mom cashed it and off to Martin Luther King Blvd we went, getting little over a bun and splitting it between us. I had gotten 4 bags and this was my first time doing it by myself and I swear to god my hands shook just like the first time I ever did dope. I had a hard time opening the bags so I tore most of them in half, a tiny amount of the powder getting on my finger tips. But the ritual came to memory after a while, and before I knew it my hands were taking the straw to my nose for me. That was that. About halfway to the mall, I was already nodding out, making Brett and Jess laugh their ass off because I'd fall asleep talking. I tried my best to sober up when we got there because Jane was highly against dope, but when I could barely keep my eyes open Jess had told her I took a Xanax.

Me, Jess, and Jen. Yeah, 'Xanax'.

A couple of nights after that is when things got really fucked up.

One night in October we robbed (my first time ever robbing someone) this girl Jojo - one of Jordan's best friend's at the time. We robbed her for 100$, saying that we could never bring the weed back to her because we got set up and arrested. They didn't believe that Brian and Jordan were locked up because they had called, apparently, 3 counties worth of police station and no one had two men by those names locked up. We called them crazy, then called it a night.

On October 13th, my Momom had given me 100$ to go see my uncle's band play at Champs, the local bar in Trenton where most shows were. I went, saw him play, got a really cool hoodie and went back to my apartment with Jordan where Brian and Christina were waiting. We got more high on this stamp called Shameless - one that even in the oncoming years I'd never see. It was purple and green and was filled to almost the second fold and just two bags got me going. I did almost all the bags that night. Around midnight I got a message from this girl Jojo, threatening my life because I had turned Jordan on to drugs. That set me off more than anything (even more than her saying she'd get me shot because that was just fucking hilarious.) We went back and forth for hours before going to sleep, and when we woke up it was the same fucking thing. Now it got to the point where Jordan was going to fight her boyfriend at the time, Mike. I was slowly figuring out that most of his stories were lies, and because I didn't want him to get beat up I said I'd fight him, too. For some reason, he was okay with his girl fighting his battles and arranged the fight.

Scott picked us up in a car packed with his new friends. This girl Paige I had known, my old friend with the basement we'd hang out in, and some random Paige I think was dating. It was October 14th, around 4:30 P.M. I brought my purse with me as always, not even thinking anything would be a problem...especially not with all the empty dope bags that were in my wallet (we kept them for scrapes.) And then, all the sudden, it happened so slowly. This stupid Attila song was on where the lyrics go "suck my dick" and one of the guys shouted them out of the window...right to a cop car. We made a left onto South Clinton, passing the high school and almost made it to the White Horse Circle and then that was it. We got pulled over.

Nobody in my family knew I was getting high. My mother had her suspicions the night I went to the mall with Jess and fell asleep into my chicken dinner, but she believed me when I told her I smoked pot. They came to our windows - 4 cops for 4 windows. They pulled Scott out of the car on suspicions he was getting high (the only thing he had ever done was drink), and when their thirst wasn't quenched with that they came to my window. "So, we think your friend Scott is high.." Officer Quick said, not giving us a chance to protest "so we're searching you because of that." I looked to my boyfriend who for some reason took all my bags out of the safe confines of my wallet and shoved them into my North Face's pockets and calmly, as best as I could say "call my momom."

My phone rang as I was getting out of the car with my one hand extended in the air, one on my pocket. "Please let me answer that, it's my mother," I begged and begged and begged, trying fucking anything for him to not search me. I was 17 and had never been in this position before, I didn't know what to do besides panic and beg. I didn't know what they were doing was a cheap ass move, I didn't know they I could've said no to a search since I was so young. I didn't know anything. So when he told me to move my hand or he'd have to take action I cried and moved it, his hands begging to pat me down. "What's in this pocket?" he asked quickly, reaching into it before I got to answer. "Just a dollar, sir" came squeaking out. "And this one?"

And that was it. He put his hand in my pockets and his eyes opened wide when he was met with the scratchy material of wax paper. "How old are you?" He whispered, getting his handcuffs out. "17" I sobbed back, giving up completely now. "You're 17 years old...and doing heroin?"

I think I said something like it's not mine, but when he asked me who's it was I quickly shut my mouth. Obviously, I couldn't be labeled a snitch, and I kind of only knew one dealer's name and it was the most common one around. I was fucked, and that was it. I was getting arrested and crying my eyes out like a little bitch for all of Hamilton to see. That was it. Everything was up, my secret was out and I'd be dead because of it. My mother would kick me out, no one would talk to me again and Scott would stop talking to me completely.

I cannot tell you the dread I felt sitting in that car through these pages. I cannot even begin to describe the feelings that were going through my body. It was worse than the time my mother found an empty dime bag of pot in my purse in the 9th grade. She'd kick me out, no doubt about it and right before she did she'd call my momom. My beautiful, angel of a grandmother would be heartbroken. For the first time in a real, real long time I had a panic attack. The car was getting hot and the doors and the cage were starting to lean in on me and I cried more. I begged like a fucking animal for the cops to open the window, I even told them the truth - I was having a panic attack. They laughed at me. They fucking laughed at me and one of them called me a loser for being "a young junkie" and I cried again. I think if I had realized they didn't read me my rights, I would've been in a lot better of shape.

Everyone else was about to leave, but before Scott left he asked why he was getting an open container ticket when the kid with the basement owned up to it being his. The officer gave no response, just yelled in his face and said "You're lucky I'm not charging you with heroin distribution." I tried to yell through the window, telling them Scott had nothing to do with it and Scott did the same but they just laughed in our fucking faces again. After another literal half hour of Scott and everyone leaving, Officer Quick got into the car. He took another five minutes and finally started to drive away, beginning the short drive to the Hamilton Police Station. I cried the whole way there. "So, has your boyfriend ever gotten locked up for drugs?" I said no, even though I knew the answer was yes. That was the only thing he had ever been honest about - how many times he'd been arrested for little amounts of weed. Before we got to the station, we stopped at the traffic light right before the building. One of the other officers who had arrested me was right next to us then, laughing along with Quick as they both revved their engines and raced towards the station. I started to dislike cops then. Arresting me for something illegal, meanwhile, you're laughing at me and illegally racing down the street? Fucking ridiculous.

They searched my purse and found more bags of dope, then asked me questions about my name and where I lived and if I had any tattoo's. I had only one at the time so I told them about it - it was a dove with my Great Grandmother Edith's name. One of them laughed and said it sounded fucking ridiculous. Quick, who started to become a lot nicer, told me I would have to call someone and I cried again. I would have to call Momom, this much I was sure of. Mommy was with Mike (her boyfriend/my stepdad I talked about earlier) and if he heard what was going on he'd not only kill me, he'd kill her, then after that, she'd take her anger out on me. "I...I..I have to call my m-momom, s-s-ir, on m-m-my phone, she won't answer if s-s-s-he doesn't recognize the number." So he gave me my phone and I called, praying to a God that probably hates me for her to answer. I didn't even give her a chance to say hello, instead just crying out "Momom, you know I wouldn't do any drugs, ever, right?" And as soon as her answer was 'no', Quick took the phone from me and told her I was arrested.

They locked one hand to a bar, leaving me to wait in a seat behind the desk until she got there. It wasn't so much of a room as it was a long hallway with a door that leads off to an interrogation room, and a long pole that they handcuffed you to that had graffiti sprawled over it. The overhead lights worked way too much, giving you a headache on top of having to sit here forever. When I have panic attacks or PTSD or my depersonalization sets in, I get this thing called compulsive skin picking. I attack ferociously at my fingertips, tearing anything that looks uneven up and never worrying about bleeding. I don't feel the hurt or the sting that is air touching open wound, I just start to feel little waves of calm rushing over me. I wish I was high right now because *oh my god* would that make everything a tiny bit better. The seconds that slowly crawled by felt like hours waiting for my momom and each minute got worse and fucking worse.

"So, here's the good news!" Quick said happily as he came out, making his way towards the person at the front desk. "We found no full bag of heroin in that whole mess of a purse. So, with that being said, your charge is downgraded to just a paraphernalia charge." Paraphernalia? That's nothing! I wouldn't go to jail over that, right? They wouldn't charge me as an adult for something so little as paraphernalia, right? I could work this out.

Soon after that Momom came through the doors and I literally screamed for her to get me out. "Not so fast, kiddo," Quick said with a laughter, bringing a bag of empties out to my grandmother. They wouldn't let me see her face or even get to protest my argument because instead they were dragging me to get my mugshot and fingerprints taken. I ran into Momom's arms after that, crying hysterically. "Like I said, ma'am, I don't think she's doing the heroin and I certainly don't think it's hers" he looked straight into my eyes then. "Are you sure this isn't your boyfriends?" I said no between sobs and Momom thanked him kindly, getting information about when I would hear from the courts then sat me down.

"I just need to ask...is this yours?" I couldn't face her eyes. Her gentle fucking eyes that would make me jump off a building right now, so all I could do was lie and say no. "Who would let you just hold 30 bags of heroin? Anyone doing that much has a problem. How are we going to tell your mother?" Perhaps it was the panic in my voice, or perhaps it was the way I cried or the way I said "I can't tell her, she'll kick me out" that made her decision, but when she said we'd hide it from her I wanted to die happy.

We left the station, picking up Jordan and cigarettes on the way home. I tore off my Northface and black skinny jeans, vowing to never ever wear them again because they were cursed. I called John who made jokes and said "so I guess you'll need money to get high with tomorrow, right? I got you." I tried to argue with him, saying I'm too afraid to get high but he didn't believe it. I hung up on him and called Jess. Jess was rolling face but sounded so fucking concerned when I told her what happened and said she had a bad feeling about me all fucking night. My boyfriend went to sleep that night and once again I was up all night. I texted my Momom apology after apology, her voice saying '*Anyone doing that much heroin has a problem*' running through my head over and over again. Why didn't I stop when I had a chance, all those nights ago at Jordan's house? Why did I want to be a part of something so bad? This didn't payoff. This made me fucking miserable. I thought about the doctor's appointment I went to a few days ago, the one I made because I felt sick, but then felt stupid going to because I felt better. I did a bag of heroin that today, a stamp called Taliban that was known for its high potency. It hit me. I was officially addicted to heroin at 17 years of age.

I didn't go to sleep well that night, and when I did fall asleep I had a bad case of night terrors.

Chapter Five

I really, truly, 100% tried to stay clean. I did really, REALLY well until the next time I got money. That's when it progressed.

"I think I wanna shoot it," I exclaimed to Jordan one day, who in exchange made his eyes turn to the size of the moon. He called me nuts, saying we'd end up just like Brian and Christina and we should stay just shooting it. "I just wanna try it once, that's it. I don't even like needles so who the fuck knows." He argued with me all the way up until Brian and Christina picked us up to cop. We were halfway down Hamilton Ave when I got a call on my cell phone. My mother. My heart dropped.

My mother hardly, if at all, called me when I was out. I knew. I fucking knew what it was about. It wasn't 5 - that's when the mail came. It wasn't a court notice, it wasn't David banging down the apartment door threatening me as he loved doing. I messed up. Somewhere under my heroin induced nods, I left an empty bag out. "Hello?"

"Tell me the truth right fucking now Kayla", she seethed through the phone, the hostility enough for even Brian and Christina to hear via front seat. "Are you doing heroin?"

I could've ended everything right there. I could've told her the truth, gone to some stupid rehab I didn't need for 90 days and that would've been the end of it. I would've never picked up again. But of course, that's not what I did. I was terrified of the outcome. What if she kicked me out? What if she told Momom who I had JUST persuaded I wasn't doing heroin, and what I got arrested for was from a party that I had tried to clean up for? Mommy would find out I was arrested. She'd beat my ass and then disown me. That'd be it.

So, I denied. I denied and denied and denied. I told her the same excuse I had told the cops and Momom - I had a party. Some kid named Jay was getting high. I forgot to throw it out. She believed it for a second...until five minutes after I copped she called me again. "Don't you DARE fucking lie to me, Kayla," she screamed, making me wince and immediately put the straw down. I was in the parking lot of Russo's, this place where all the local music kids went for

guitars and drums and shit like that. We sometimes went when
Brian and my boyfriend wanted to practice their acoustic songs.
"Your fucking room is filled with empty dope baggies. Jordan's
clothes, your fucking drawer! It's a fucking drug den in here Kayla."

She went on a fucking rampage, searching through his and mine's
clothes, ripping our drawers and clothes out of my closet. When it
was happening, I thought she was a fucking psychopath and told
her so, only making my situation worse. Now, a few years later, I
don't blame her. I'd do the same fucking thing if that was going on in
my apartment. Again, I lied. I lied but told her that this was the real
truth. I blamed it on my friends. "D-d-o you remember the night, I
had friends over? A-a-and you k-knocked on my door b-because
there was so much s-smoke?" I sobbed out, trying to keep her as
calm as I could. A few days ago a couple people came over to get
high with me and Jordan who by this time was mooching a free
place to live with me. My mother got mad because the whole
apartment was smokey from cigarette after cigarette. She said yes,
she indeed did remember that night, then burst out crying. She
believed me. I cried too, saying I was sorry for being so dumb, I just
wanted friends. That part was true, at least.

By the time the conversation had ended, we ended up at the park
across the Morrisville Bridge, Castle Park I think it was called. Brian
and Christina gave us a couple Xanax to snort, saying they're sorry
and that we'll get through this. Brian gave Jordan a lesson in life,
saying to be strong for me. Christina told me the story about when
her parents found a bunch of dope in her room, too.

That day came and went. My addiction became worse as I had
found a new dealer named Sky who lived off of Stuyvesant. I had
met him when I copped with Max. His boy was doing the deal and
used my phone to call his dude. Most addicts delete their dealer's
number, so you can't go through the actual dealer but instead use
the addict as a middleman so he'd get some profit. The day after,
though, his dealer called me. I did it. I finally had my own fucking
dealer I wouldn't need a middleman for shit unless they were driving
me. People would give *me* bags. They'd owe me shit. I did it.

Right before that, however, was Hurricane Sandy. I don't know if
any of you remember it or not, but in New Jersey, it struck my area
with a frightening force. I could only get two bags - two bags given to
me by Brian and Christina. Christina somehow got money out of her
grandfather, saying she needed it for a doctor's appointment but he

knew that she was getting high. So, one step ahead of her, he wrote a check out. Christina, the addict she was, was one step ahead of him. She told him to write it out to Dr. Jordan Bierz. Yes. She used his name as her doctor. So, in return for signing the check, we would get two bags.

I had never seen bags like this, either. They were all purple, and in a black stamp said 'Game over' and had a Gameboy imprinted on them. I knew I wouldn't get high, I was fucking terrified my run down apartment would get destroyed in the hurricane, and my PTSD was acting up like it did every Halloween because of the shit that happened with my dad...so I did it. I shot up for the first time on October 30th. I wanted to quiet my PTSD. I wanted the panic to stop. I wanted to be high.

Jordan went first. It was quick. By the time Brian was mixing up my shit, an almost ritualistic act, Jordan was leaning on the door, mumbling to himself. I freaked the fuck out. "Am I gonna feel like that? I don't want to." I panicked, scooting as far away from the needle as I could.

"No, absolutely not," Brian said between laughs of irritation. "He's just being dramatic as usual." Christina agreed. "Don't even look at him, he's being a fucking idiot."

I swallowed hard and nodded, holding my skinny pale arm out for Brian to find a vein.

Unlike most doctors (because addicts are always better), Brian found one quick. I was getting dizzy watching as he began to tie me up.

"I...I think I might pass out."

"Don't fucking look, then." He whispered harshly, slowly putting the tip of the needle in my arm. I was getting too hot, I wanted to cry. I hated this shit so much.

I didn't feel any warmth, in fact I felt no euphoria either. I just felt my head get dizzy...then that was it. I passed out. I woke up a few seconds later as Brian was recapping his needle and Christina was packing her shit up.

"I thought you were having a fucking seizure by the noises you were making" my boyfriend panicked, "we all thought you were dead!"

I looked at the scene before me. They thought I was dead..yet they were packing their shit up to leave? Christina was practically halfway out the door. They were going to leave me to fucking die. "I'm fine. Thanks." I snapped, pulling my sleeve down. I asked them to leave at that point, annoyed. How dare they think that's okay? They were in *my* fucking house, getting high on money that *I* helped them get, as usual. I looked to Jordan's face, and I guess he was thinking the same thing as me because he whispered to let it go. I was annoyed with him, too.

That night was spent watching movies and making sure I didn't bend my arm the wrong way. I was mad I didn't get high, I kinda just fell asleep here and there. It was like in the summer time when John would give us 6 Tramadol each, along with an anti-seizure medicine. "*Trust me, sis. It'll get you fucked up.*" I didn't know much so I believed him, mad when it did nothing. I just couldn't pee and fell asleep everywhere, no euphoria in sight. If this was what shooting up was, I fucking hated it.

It was November now, that night forgotten about unless I was telling the tale. The air was bitter against skin, money was slightly harder to get from Momom because I could no longer use the excuse of going to Seaside or the beach in general. I was robbing everyone I could, now. The kid that helped me get those 3 bags back in September? Robbed for 50$. I gave him a fake G-Shock I picked up somewhere and gave it to him, telling him I had to be back because I needed my watch. I never came back. Another jux I was doing was getting leftover birth control and saying they were Roxy's, that was the most profitable. One time Jordan sold fake Roxy's to a guy in a hospital - dude apparently cut an artery and they wouldn't give him any pain meds so he came to us, and our sad asses robbed him blind.

I now also understood what it meant to be dope sick. There was nothing like it in the fucking world. People told me it was like a 'more intense flu' and I guess they were right - besides the fact there's a five dollar fucking cure for it and I milked all my options dry. I hated smoking - I only had it in me to take a few pulls before throwing the thing half way across the room. If air brushed against my skin it stung, and I hardly could gather enough strength to get up from my toilet. My relationship was going to shit, too. I hated being around him. I hated his lies, I hated how he'd sing in his high-pitch voice all around the apartment. The neighbors would make fun of him and I would too. We started fighting more and more, sometimes about who got more dope, sometimes just to fight. I hated how submissive he was. One night we couldn't get dope because Brian and Christina couldn't get the car, so he thought it'd be a good idea to hit up David.

A few minutes later he was at my door, 5 month old baby and Marie in hand. She and I greeted each other with fake 'hellos' and 'I missed yous', meanwhile my boyfriend got out his binder full of stupid stories and showed them while we waited for their dealer. The baby was gorgeous, there was no doubt about that and she was *good*. If anyone could conjure up an image of a perfect, well behaved child this was it. I was sick and bought a bag off of them for 10$ instead of 5$, knowing they were ripping me off but too sick to care. Finally their dealer couldn't make it to my apartment so instead they had to go to Stuyvesant. I had to wait at home with the baby who was now asleep on my couch, instructions on how to make a bottle swimming in my brain.

How did I end up here? How did I end up a 17 year old heroin addict, watching the two people who had hurt me the most at that point's baby? Why wasn't as mad as I should be? Maybe I was slowly growing and I wasn't capable of such hate as I previously was. Maybe the three month of every day heroin abuse jaded me, or maybe I truly just didn't give a fuck and started to worry about my own problems. Maybe this was adulthood.

The three of them returned a short while later and off we went to snorting off any clear surface. They hadn't been shooting yet, either, but we told them about the one night during Hurricane Sandy and they had said they wanted to try it once.

After awhile they finally left, saying that we'd hang out later and I reluctantly agreed. One time we got Xanax off them, trading them 5 cigarettes for it. Another time we couldn't get dope, Brian and Christina didn't want to come out to Trenton that day so we hit them up. They said they were going to Camden now, and when they got back they'd hit us up. After awhile it was 7 PM and I was dancing out of my fucking skin, blowing their phones up to get no response. In the world of drug addiction, you go to who has it first, not who you made promises to because *that was just silly.* Brian and Christina finally came, and David called around then. I told him the truth - we already copped because we didn't want to wait.

"Alright, bet, fine, watch what happens. Watch what happens when I get my ruby red's on you. Watch what happens when I get my gun and come to your fucking house, Kayla. Watch what happens when you come home to find your mother gone and yellow tape in her fat fucking place."

I lost it. No more was the little 15 year old girl who would bend to his every will, but a human fucking being with feelings who wasn't taking shit - being threatened by a gun and a gang or not. I didn't understand the big deal - I hadn't even given them any money to cop...it's not like they went out of their way since they were going to Camden anyway. I had no part of it, I was just someone who needed dope if they had extra. If I had known that I could've just easily called the cops, or that no gang or no gun was going to be brought to my house, I probably would've just hung up. But instead like a pawn I played into it, fueling his anger like he loved. We all rushed to my house and I told my mother the story, telling her to just stay asleep and we'd handle it. Jordan was already yapping away, saying he'd fuck him up but my mother quickly stopped that and said to leave it alone.

Brian was the one, who in fact, waited outside my house for any sign of them. They drove up to the building, asked his name, and that was it. The most they did that night was threaten and make themselves look like idiots. The last one to talk was Marie, saying that it was my fault the baby would go hungry, and if they got arrested for shoplifting baby formula it would be on me.

But who the fuck lets their child go hungry to buy dope, anyway?

The next night was the same, and I was out with Jess and Brent and Brett and Jordan. At around midnight my mother called me in a panic, and I could hear the bangs on the door through the phone. She was scared and had every reason to be, she had no idea what was going on. I told her the truth -David was mad I wouldn't give him money. I came home that night to find my neighbors on the porch, saying it was fine as I apologized for the knocking. They didn't care, they instead thought it was funny how they drove off in their tiny red ford fusion. We stopped talking for awhile after that.

Thanksgiving came, and I had never been higher. My dad had picked me up and I would see my grandparents for the first time in a year since they had moved to Florida. We went to my Aunt Rhonda's in Manalapan, both of us getting money and calling our dealers. He told me his was for weed...I told him I was going to the movies. We both knew, I think. I copped through Jess, hung out with her for a little while we watched *Twilight* and that was it. For the first time in my whole heroin addiction, I was completely alone. No boyfriend, no mother in the next room….just me and my cat, Foxxy Cleopatra. I was free to snort lines off the coffee table in the living room and I did that. I nodded out in the peace of my own apartment, no one to bother me or to say otherwise. I smoked cigarettes back-to-back and didn't split them with anybody, and if I was hungry I ate whipped cream and loved it.

The world was finally quiet and I finally felt apart of it. No longer did I feel like I was always in a movie, or that everyone was fake and I was the only real living person with emotions. I finally felt fucking free and I never wanted to be locked in the chains that is mental illness again. I wanted to live like this forever, even if it meant I had to be sick. I didn't care. This is all I had ever wanted - a quiet mind, a feeling of fitting in on Earth.

Like everything, the dope and the high comes and goes - as soon as I felt like that it was gone, never to reach my fingertips again. I hated it.

My mother found a lot more empty bags of heroin and out of my mouth came a lot more lies, too. I swore they weren't mine and I swore I was holding onto them because my friends were scared their parents would kick them out and I knew my mother wouldn't because *she was understanding.* It would break my heart to lie to her and to see her cry..until I got high.

David got locked up. Someone had called DYFS on him and Marie because they were now shooting up and way too into their addiction to be functioning parents. He got three months and I was upset because that's what kind of sick relationship we had. Something bad would happen and I'd cry my fucking heart out - something bad would happen to me and he'd laugh. Jordan didn't care, ever. In fact he was out cheating on me, the only way I knew was via his Facebook messages inbox he would never clean out. There was always a new girl every single day. One time I found out before we went to cop, and instead of going home with me he went to Max's - I took all the dope and did it. I got too high and scared and I had to call them to come help me. They almost broke my door down, finding me in my own vomit with a cigarette burning into my wrist. I still have the scars, and that's one thing I miss the most: numbing my pain.

I started to feel some kid named Jason. We got high together and he was calmer than Jordan, more mature. We liked each other and that lasted for awhile until some bullshit happened and he threatened to show texts to my boyfriend saying how much I hated him. Jason broke up with his girlfriend, this girl Kelsey, and she found out about the whole thing too. For awhile, probably to this day even, her claws became hooked into Jordan. Even though I had somebody that made sure to tell me how much he loved me, so much so to the point he'd cry and block doors so I wouldn't leave him, I was lonely. Nobody understood me but heroin. I had no friends besides Jess, but Jordan shot her up for the first time and that was it - she was hooked harder than ever. She was gone after that night. I was the only one snorting, besides Jordan on the occasions he'd do it in front of me and lie and say he wasn't shooting up. I'd find the track marks inside the shallows of his arms.

It was funny in some sort of sick, cruel way. The thing that brought me closer to all of these people was only making me isolated.

Some nights weren't always terrible. The day usually started off with either having bags or not, then progressed to doing them, then to getting money. I either got money from my Momom, on the rare my mother, or we robbed someone. Then, we'd find a ride from someone, anyone. It was either Brian and Christina, Jess, or maybe this kid Andrew and his brother Wesley who I couldn't stand. One time Wesley picked us up, and they were going to a dude off of Stuyvesant who had these bags called Sleepwalker or some shit - I hated them. I thought they were poopoo and asked to take us to our dude Sky since he was only a street over. He said no because Sky robbed him and if he sees him he's 'gonna knock him the fuck out.' I guess he didn't like that I laughed in his face, but to relieve the situation Andrew said he'd just call his other guy. Lo and behold, his guy shorted us a few bags and Wesley still wanted four. He *really* didn't like when I laughed in his face then, because he pulled over on '29 and tried to get me out of the car. I threatened his girlfriend and they took us home.

I hardly ever got robbed because I was so paranoid...and so close to my dealers (or so I and every other addict in the world thought.) I counted each and every single bag out and made sure I was handed them as soon as we were driving away. I talked a lot of shit, too, and I think because people didn't want to deal with it they mostly gave me my way. Christina robbed me for 2 bags once, then later for a lot of money. I looked for her every day for weeks after that.

Christmas time was a little nicer. It was around the anniversary of my friend's death so I was crying a lot, and on top of that my wisdom teeth were coming in. I was a lot angrier; a lot harder to control. I wasn't happy unless I had dope, and the stress I put on my mother or even my cheating boyfriend was getting hard for them. I didn't have a job and everyone was sick of handing me money, and the amount of fights I got into on Facebook for owing people money was insane. I didn't drive, or even have a license, my friends were wondering why I was always sleepy - I had spiraled out of control and didn't care. As long as I was high, I was happy...until I got my court date in the mail.

I got arrested on October 14th and here it was, Christmas fucking Eve and I finally got my letter. I thought they had forgotten about me, honestly. I thought it was over and done with because Officer Quick put a word in that they weren't mine. I quickly hid the letter in my hoodie and ran to my room, showing it to Jordan who was playing a stupid RPG on his iPod touch. "You said I wouldn't get this" I lowly yelled, ripping the parchment out of the envelope. "I'm fucked. I'm going to jail. This is it."

He rolled his eyes. "You're going to be fine, I promise. I got caught with paraphernalia and just got some probation."

The difference between that, however, was it was a small amount of weed. This, according to Quick and the court papers, was exactly 32 glassine bags of heroin and intent to distribute - that was a new one.

"Piece of shit lied to me. I'll just use my thing, that thing that you can use when you've never been locked up!!" PTE - pre trial intervention. A first offender's best friend, and now it was going to be mine. Before they even got to ask me any questions I was just going to slam that on them and be done, no jail time or anything.

"Yeah, just use that babe you'll be alright. It's really not even a big deal." It wasn't a big deal to him because he didn't get arrested. Half of those fucking things were his, anyway - I just took the blame because he'd 'apparently go back to jail.' Yeah, right. He was just a pussy and didn't think.

I texted my Momom, and told her the news. All she replied with was a simple 'we'll handle it.' I hoped we'd do just that. I thought about my Popop Puppy - my mom's dad (he and momom were divorced. To make it easier on me because I had three sets of grandparents, they each had their own nickname. Momom was just my regular, see her every day momom. Momom Taco bell, named because we had a dog named Taco Bell, was my dad's mother. Popop Puppy was because he had a puppy. Smart, right?) and how we would react if he ever found out. He threatened to kick me out of our house over an empty dime bag of pot when I was 14. His wife, my step-momom, worked with the Courts or something like that and could easily look my name up to see what I've been doing. If they ever found out, I would just have to tell them the truth. I would go to a rehab or a psych ward or something, anything. I didn't want to be homeless. I didn't want to go through this anymore.

On New Year's Eve, I got into my first physical fight with Jordan. I found out in between waiting for dealers (because our main one had robbed Brian and Christina, something I was very happy about because I'm petty) that he had been messaging girls for nudes. What a time to be alive, right? I asked to see the messages, over and over and over; I fucking begged. He wouldn't give it up so I did what any rational person would do: punch him. I punched him and probably said something along the corny lines of "I'll knock you the fuck out, pussy." New Year's Eve was turning out horrible. We had no dealer, they had no car for the night, and I hated everything.

"Why don't we just ask Sky to take a cab?" I said through a mouth full of chicken, immediately embarrassed of the idea. "I have like, 100. We'll just get 80 worth and pay him 20 for a cab."

No one else thought it was a ridiculously horrible idea, either, because we all had Jordan call him. He said okay and it was like a fucking angel had blessed us, however sick that may be. He came to the Dunkin Donuts by my house in no time AND had given us 2 buns, with a little extra. When we got back to the safe confines of my 'drug den' of a room, I immediately started opening bags. Brian and Christina looked like children who had just gotten scolded, knowing they had no reason to get some. They didn't give us a ride, they didn't bring us to their dealer, D. They were fucked. I loved it. I loved watching the sorrow in their face; the hurt of knowing that they might be sick for longer than they had planned. This is what they did to us; to me. They took and took and took until there was nothing left and they were finally getting what they deserved. I loved it. As petty of a person I can be, the anger I held took me back. They were lonely drug addicts, too. They got sick and had to rob and lie and thief to get well, too. Their addiction made them like this, not their actual personalities. I sighed, and before I could open my mouth Jordan was already handing them 4 bags each - *that* I wasn't going to do, but okay I guess.

The rest of the night we hung out with my mom in the living room because her boyfriend/my almost stepdad Mike had bailed on picking her up, trying to lift her spirits up with funny jokes but really not making a dent in her mood. I tried my best to not make her feel like a third wheel in her own home, making sure I sat with her and made jokes and took pictures with her. I thought it really helped until right after the ball dropped - after we kissed our significant others I heard her cry in the bathroom. It broke my heart. I always felt responsible for helping my mother, whether it be when she owed people money for Adderall or with bills or anything at that. When I couldn't help it took a chunk out of my soul, leaving me dying on the floor with my last wish to help. I guess I was always like that - helping until I had nothing left to give.

Christina left, leaving Brian to sleep over by himself. Apparently her family had found out they had maxed two credit cards out in her mother's name - the blame ultimately on Brian because they didn't want to blame their oldest daughter, or that's what I heard anyway. It didn't help her case much when the police came barging in Christina's house, taking her out by handcuffs because she got caught doing a B&E on someone's house. Her parents started to supervise her then, checking her purse and shit like that. He gave us Xanax and told us about his problems, I nodded out in between saying 'mmhm' and 'that's crazy.'

I remember being excited for the new year - the four of us made a pact to get clean and we really, really meant it. We were going to do our last bags on January 1st, 2013 and that be it. No harm would be done. We did exactly just that, and when Brian left that night we even made a pillow and blanket fort and I had so much fun doing it, saying that I'm going to sleep in the coolest thing for three days to get rid of withdrawal. Of course, that lasted up until about 3 days before I had court - just in case they drug tested me. I did really, really good - until I took some methadone I found the day off. I cried my fucking eyes out while chugging cranberry juice, hoping it would flush some of it out.

Chapter Six

It was January 14th - exactly three months since I was arrested. I wasn't that sick, in help from the methadone, so I was just shaking at that point from panic. I looked into the mirror that was attached to my dresser, staring at my face and messy room behind it. Who was I? Not the same Kayla from six months ago.

Replacing my tan skin was now an over pale, greyish color. I decided to wear my black hair straight and though it had gotten longer, it was no longer bouncy - just wavey and turning lifeless. I had gotten really skinny over the time of my breakup to pre-dope, but now I could see hip bones when I walked; when I slept I saw ribs during each inhale. Most of the time, probably because I was high, I thought I looked amazing. Tonight, I cried instead. I thought I was the most hideous person in the world. I was no longer the person people came to for advice (except for the select few who I didn't see often who couldn't tell the change in me), instead I had become the person who's Facebook I'd lurk for the latest drama. I remember thinking people who did drugs and got into fights and didn't give a fuck about anything were cool, and now that I was living and breathing in that lifestyle I hated it. I wasn't ready. I still lived off of the state's insurance, I couldn't adult yet if I tried.

Before I left the house my mother asked where I was going dressed so nice. My mother, my beautiful asshole of a mother. More and more lately she had found empty dope bags, and every single time she would cry her beautiful green-blue eyes out - I would cry with her. I couldn't afford to give her money or even stay awake to watch her stupid ghost hunting shows that she loved so much with her because instead I had chosen a drug that had ruined her life over her. Instead I was riding around Trenton buying heroin from shady drug dealers, risking my life every day and not giving a single care about it. *Well, at least I only shot dope once - you can't die from snorting it.* Right, as if.

"Just a modeling meeting, mommy," I said, holding back tears. I had just started modeling - a stupid little thing, but it made me feel sort of better about myself. "They want to talk to us about having to pay monthly dues. I'm going to fight it because it's really dumb."

"Oh my god, Kayla, that's ridiculous!" She agreed immediately. "Yeah, definitely stand up for that. I was afraid this would happen, but I don't get why they would make you a portfolio with no charge if they were going to pull this?" Her light eyebrows furrowed, trying to figure out the scenario in her head. I couldn't help but laugh at her childlike self. That was her in a nutshell.

"Well, I love you," I replied back, kissing her on the cheek before leaving. "Keep the door unlocked, I can't find my keys." She called something out, probably something about me finding my keys, but I was already hurrying into Momom's car.

"Hi, baby." She greeted, her smile sincere. "Are you ready?"

"No," I choked out, "I'm scared."

We arrived at the building about ten minutes later. It was a huge, three story red bricked building that made you feel small as soon as you parked. Juvenile Court Committee - those were the people who were deciding my fate. A 'committee' of people who got bored at jury duty and saw the advertisement of the whole thing and thought *'wow, what a good idea! I love deciding young people's fate!'* My anger was obviously no secret because in no time Momom was pulling me into a hug, telling me we'd be okay. "No matter what, we'll work this out."

You wouldn't even notice the building unless you were summoned to it. There were no lights beside the one that showcased the Grounds For Sculpture statue that stood right in front of it; a perfect statue of an elderly man reading a newspaper. I'd point it out every time I drove past it, dope in my system or not.

They didn't have an elevator, instead they had three sets of raggedy old stairs. The service elevator for employees only, the security guard had said - Momom had to drag me by the sleeve so I wouldn't continue to talk shit to him. I helped her up each stair, no complaint in me as we took our time. There was already a family there - a father, a mother, and a son - dressed to the nines in suits and beautiful dresses. I looked down at my outfit - a shitty little white button up top with black skinny jeans - the same ones I had gotten arrested in. So much for bad luck.

The family went in..then out. They spoke in whispers, a few words escaping in yells. My Momom - as always - was the first to speak.

"Are they in a good mood?" She whispered, leaning over me to be closer to the family. "Are they being forgiving tonight?

The son shrugged. "Kinda." "What do they look like?" "One's a real old lady," he began. "Real, real old. Besides that, they're dressed in like regular clothes. They seemed kinda okay, i'unno."

She was pleased with that answer. "Thanks, good luck." The family started to pray, either to avoid talking to us or because I was a hysterical mess I'm not sure, but I did too. I prayed. I prayed long and hard as to make no mistakes - I wanted to miss nothing. I prayed for my situation - that if I were in trouble, please let probation be the strongest punishment. I prayed for forgiveness, not only from God himself but from my Momom, my mother. I wanted their pain gone because the strong walls they put up didn't hide it from me. I let tears run down my face without caring, and Momom gasped. "You must be real scared if you're praying, huh?" she chuckled. "I'll pray with you."

We prayed until they called me in. It was a cramped little room - so cramped they had to move the desk back so Momom could get in. The little old lady was front and center, she'd be the lead. I didn't really notice anybody else, next to her was a little Hispanic women with short hair in her thirties. Their faces blended together; one big monster looming down at me, deciding my fate was the only thing I saw. They began with simple questions, my name, where I lived. Do I work and when's my birthday - are you in agreement that we are here to pick the best suitable action for your decisions? I nodded, and began the story Momom and I made up on the way here.

My best friend, the one driving, picked my boyfriend and me up.

"Where is your boyfriend now?" one of the monsters faces interrupted, and I shrugged.

"He's at his house, I think. He doesn't have a phone, and his house doesn't have wifi, so we don't have a way to talk." They wrote that down and I continued. I didn't know anyone in the car, so when they yelled the 'suck my dick' part of the song out of the window to the cop, I panicked.

"Was it actually a part of the song? Because that's a horrible song!" The old lady exclaimed, making Momom agree and myself chuckle, but I treaded on. We got pulled over, and automatically everyone started freaking out. What were they gonna do? How were they gonna hide shit?

"They asked me to do it, to hide it," I whispered, confident in my acting. All addicts are perfect liars. "They started to shove it in my pockets, telling my boyfriend they'd beat him up if he said anything. The girl in the front seat said something too, so I was scared. I did what we were told."

In reality, it was a perfect lie. I was actually kind of upset I didn't think of it first. They wrote every single word down, jotting down notes here and there whenever I would break out crying or if I shifted in my seat.

"Okay, well, take a seat back in the waiting room. We'll be with ya in five minutes, sweetie!" We thanked them, probably way too much, and took our leave.

"I think it went good," Momom said nonchalantly, amusement in her voice. "I really think you'll be fine."

I didn't. I was prepared for the worst. I checked my phone, Jess had just texted me words of encouragement and to make sure I knew she'd pick me up as soon as I was done. I didn't know if I would ever be done, though. I was positive they'd take me out in handcuffs and lock away the key, my poor grandmother to be the only one who kind of knew the truth.

Five minutes felt like five hours. Another family came up, this time not so well dressed. Their son sat down, fixing his fitted to be brim backward, legs sprawling outward before him. I made eye contact with his mother. She was fucking exhausted. The bags under her eyes did her no justice, they only helped in aiding her look as worn out as I'm sure she felt. His dad yelled at him, telling him this wasn't a game. The son simply replied, saying "I don't give a fuck."

My great grandmother is probably rolling in her grave if she's looking over me - not that I'd blame her if she wasn't. I wasn't what I was supposed to be. I was supposed to know the dangers of addiction, especially after my childhood, and never pick anything up. I was always smart - I was supposed to take that John Hopkin's scholarship I got in 8th grade and go all the way to the top, not drop out of high school at 16 to party and do ecstasy. I was supposed to go to Princeton, be a vet, marry a nice Jewish boy - and here I am, crying my eyes out on a wooden bench in juvenile court. Why did life move so fast?

"Okay, Kayla, you can come back in" the little Hispanic lady called, her hand motioning to come in the room. I braced myself for the worst. This was it.

They all looked at me, faces now separating into actual bodies and not just a cluster of one. "For Kayla Small, in action to her arrest on October 14th, 2012, with a count of paraphernalia and intent to distribute...we order for two days community service, the last two Sunday's of April."

"Oh my god, no way." Their faces turned light, smiling at my reaction. How did I do this? Am I really that fucking good of a liar? I didn't even have to say names! I didn't even snitch! Is this because Officer Quick put his opinion down too, stating he believed they weren't mine? I did it. I did it, I did it, I did it. I would be safe to go to my apartment, kiss my mother's face and lay with my cat for the rest of my life if I wanted to.

"Please start hanging out with better people, not one's with bad addiction problems, and no bullies!" The little old lady said, writing down the days I would have to go to my community service. I promised her I wouldn't, my Momom and I thanking them all for their kindness a thousand times over.

I did it. I would only have to go to Trenton's soup kitchen and help feed the homeless...twice! I got away! My record would be expunged when I turned 18 and no one would know this ever happened. I don't know what higher power helped me out, but I guess God really was listening to me. I practically danced out of that building, calling Jess to tell her I was free. Momom overheard me, offering to give me money and buy me food before we went home. My angel. My savior.

I called Jess again, telling her to pick me up - I needed a bun. I needed to celebrate.

Chapter Seven

January 2013.

Life went by too fast. Every day passed before me in a drug induced haze, everything kind of mixing together.

I had to get my wisdom teeth taken out - that much I knew and was terrified of. I went to the dentist's office, my mother and Aunt Jen walking behind me as I signed myself in. This was it, I couldn't turn back now. I saw person after person walk out of the back, staggering and drooling on themselves and I hated it - who would want to feel like that? *Not like I was doing much else on dope.* A lady called me back, a plump little thing that I would eventually meet later via the huge crush she had on my now husband. She lead me to the surgeon's office, a nice older white guy who was overly flamboyant. I sat down, taking my signature *Sicker Than Most* hoodie I got from my Uncle's show back in October off, turning my eyes away as they had to find a vein for the valium they'd use to knock me out.

"That's a pretty uh..mighty scar you got there." He was trying to find the right words without coming out and saying 'what happened?'. I told him it was a burn.

"A burn?" His eyebrows raised to his hairline.

"Yeah, I burnt myself with a cigarette, wasn't really paying atten-Owwww." The assistant found a vein, quickly inserting the valium drip before I had a chance to complain anymore.

"Well, it must've been on there for a real long time to get that.." He said something, but I couldn't hear him. I was already knocking out into valium land. Benzo's were pretty cool, especially if you were on dope. On the same hand, I've seen more and more people die from that lethal cocktail than anything and I'd stop anyone in the world from mixing if I could - except when I was 17 and went to get four wisdom teeth pulled out, a bundle of heroin in my system about to make out with veins full of valium.

I came out loopy as fuck but biting my tongue, making sure I said everything *but* the fact I went to court and my heroin addict. I'd hide them but let everything else slide. Did Mommy and Aunt Jen know how excited I was that they were here? Well, they do now! Did the girl who brought me in the doctor's room know she was my 'number one homie', and that I'd chill with her *every. Single. Day*?! She sure as fuck did now.

I was even excited to see Jordan as I walked in my apartment door - was he always this great? He had to be.

"Hi, baby!" I said excitedly, taking a blanket from my room and tossing it on the couch. "I'm home! I feel great! I don't know why I was so scared! I don't even hurt!"

That lasted like a fucking hour.

Momom had given us 40$ - money to get food while I still felt good, she said. Brian and Christina couldn't come through for whatever fucking reason, Jess was ignoring me, and I almost threw a fit before a message on Facebook popped up. David.

He'd just gotten out of jail and didn't want to go back home yet - he wanted to get high for a little bit so he did just that. He came to my apartment, my mother greeting him happily and Jordan doing the same. I said hi, taking out bloody gauze piece by piece so I could smoke. The two of them walked, my upstairs neighbor commenting that they must be fucking crazy to hang out together - he'd never let his girls ex anywhere near the two of them.

I shrugged. "Yeah, they're fucking weirdos."

He slept over that night and left, then I copped from Christina and Brian. It took me four days to do that bundle - a new feat seeing as a bundle was gone in six hours if that. I hardly touched it. I took the Percocet the doctor gave to me and lyed on the couch, throwing up every five minutes. I was fucking miserable. Jordan would leave and do whatever the fuck he wanted, not caring if I was sick or not. I found out by a mutual friend he was at the mall with that girl Kelsey - to stop me from bugging out he promptly told me he robbed her for 80$. I got high to ignore the ache in my chest.

I got a job at the local Outback Steakhouse and without having to say, I fucking hated it. I hated the girls who worked the hostess stand with me - preppy girls from Bordentown who had their whole lives handed to them. I made really, really good money for an addict, too. I usually brought home 60$ in tips each night and usually made 80$ every payday. Thinking back now, I could've sued the fuck outta them. It would be Kayla's Steakhouse or something corny like that. I was 17, getting sexually harassed every day I went in ('oh, girl, you are just killing me in that shirt' or 'oh girl, they hate you because you're the hottest one here, just look at yourself.'), working 8 hour shifts and got no breaks. I don't know why my dope head mentality didn't pick this up - I would've been rich. I could've swum in seas of glassine baggies.

That job lasted maybe three weeks, even though I convinced myself I was functioning. I just never came in one day, the only hint of me being fired was them updating my schedule to no days. I thought it was fucking hysterical, as did everyone else.

It was now tax return season time - a beautiful, beautiful day. I myself could not collect, seeing as my first job at Hamilton Diner misspelled my name as "Kaya Simou", but my mother could. She'd get extra money for claiming me as a dependant, too - making 200$ mine. Although I can hardly fucking remember that night, it was one of my favorites.

Jess and Brett came and so did Brian and Christina. We bought dope on dope upon dope, getting high in my living as my mother didn't come home until 5 - or so I thought. Around 4:30 I emptied a bag out, some nonchalant stamp I paid no attention to. The straw was already in my nose, and right as I was about to breathe in...the door unlocked. My fucking mother.

"It's a party in here, huh?" She joked as everyone's pinned iris' looked at me. I gently placed my Pink Floyd wallet in my purse, the straw going in the side pocket of it as I greeted her. I probably didn't help my case as I carefully tip-toed to the bathroom, making sure as to make no movement strong enough to knock the line out of place. I snorted it and walked out, my mother meeting me in the long hallway.

"Kay...what were you doing?"

"A Xanax," I replied back, taking one out of my back pocket. Thanks, Christina, I really owed you one right now. "See?"

She believed me. In fact, up until she probably just read that, she believed me. Sorry, Mommy.

We went to the mall, everyone stealing whatever they could put their hands on as I kind of just stood in the background not doing much of anything. I looked at clothes here and there, went to various stores but never really did anything. I was too scared to steal, honestly. Besides that, my mom had given me enough money to go shopping with, too - I was set.

Jess came out the mall with the fucking works: skinny jeans that she actually gave me, band t-shirts and a whole new fucking outfit. She even got a beanie to match the brand new one I got.

Taylor and Christina were the same, bras from Victoria's Secret and somehow even a North face. I was amazed. They gave me my first bombshell, a cute little lacy pink and cheetah print thing that I still have to this day. Anytime I put it on, I think about that night.

The next day was different.

My mother gave me another 100 - I told her I'd be going out later and wanted to buy pot (and she was always very giving when she got her taxes.) I didn't want to go to Stuyvesant with Brian, Christina, Taylor, and Jordan so I opted to stay home, giving him the money with very clear instructions. We were to buy 18 bags, and they were to get only 4 - nothing more. I'd count them when they got here and if anything was iffy, we'd fight. He said okay, he even agreed then took my Taco Bell order and left, kissing me before leaving.

Hour one came up. To get to Stuyvesant from my house, it took maybe ten minutes IF that. I knew something was up, but I had no phone to call - they took mine. I was stuck sick, waiting on my couch while I dodged questions from my mom. The thoughts going through my head were getting worse by the second. What if they got arrested, what if they got tainted dope?

Eventually, they showed up. They had to, Brian had nowhere to go and Christina's parents were not letting him in. I was furious. I didn't want him in my house, my mother was getting more and more sick of him by the minute, and they took way too long. I wanted to get high in the confines of my own private bedroom, not with Brian sitting on the floor constantly asking for more bags.

Nonetheless, I said okay. My mother angered but I once again brushed it off, not really caring anymore. Brian was exceptionally nice, handing us peach Xanax's here and there and making jokes. Thinking back now, that was probably apart of his plan. He watched carefully where I hid my money, his plan circulating in only his head. I probably should've known something was up when he deleted all his messages to Christina.

I probably should've known something was up the next day, too. He got 80$ when we were sleeping, took my phone, and met with a 'new' dealer that met him a block down from my apartment. I didn't think of anything as he handed us both a bag each of Sleepwalker - ew.

By the time it was dark, Christina and Taylor came. We were all sitting in my room watching Brian and Jordan practice their acoustic shit when something happened. I don't remember what, but Jordan had to get up for a second and go in the kitchen. I went to the bathroom.

Number one rule of having heroin addicted friends is to obviously never, ever leave them with your stuff. I trusted them though, they were different; they had the whole opportunity to rob my house and they never did. Besides, I was Christina's only real girlfriend and Brian had known Jordan for years...why would they do anything?

I got back from the bathroom and they were suddenly leaving, saying how their mom needed them back asap and they didn't want to anger her. Whatever, fine, bye. I didn't care.

I didn't notice right away. In fact, the only thing I noticed was the fresh track mark in the hollow of my boyfriend's arm. My heart broke right then and there, ensuing a two hour fight with me breaking shit and punching his brace-ridded face. I only calmed down when I had to pull his cheek apart from his teeth, feeling sorry but unable to express it.

The night ended with him robbing someone with our signature fake Molly, aka sugar and salt for the bitter taste. We went to sleep happy, listening to silly Pierce The Veil songs and reminiscing our first time going to Warped Tour together and how we saw them. For once, I didn't hate being around him. For once, I wasn't completely annoyed.

I woke up the next morning sick as a fucking dog, barely able to find my bags and do them. I asked Jordan to go in my jewelry box and get ten dollars out, I really wanted real coffee, not the instant we had to drink since he broke our coffee maker trying to fix it.

"The money isn't here," he stated matter-of-factly, shuffling around various drawers.

"What the fuck do you mean, Jordan? Where the fuck could it be?" I knew it. I fucking knew it before I even had to think about it. They stole my money. The brief 30 seconds I was gone from my room, they stole 120$. They didn't care about friendship, they didn't care if we'd be sick or not...they cared about them. I was so fucking good to them, always helping out when I shouldn't, always making to go the extra mile, always making sure to cop through them because they'd be *oh so sick* without those two fucking bags in their syringe.

I lost it. I blacked out and I fucking lost it.

The first thing to be touched in my rampage was my dresser drawers. I ripped them out of their oak sockets, throwing them to the ground and made Jordan check my clothes. Maybe, for some reason, I hid them in old jean's pocket because no dope head ever would suspect that, right? Maybe I just misplaced it. I know I didn't, but maybe during the fight last night or maybe during a nod out session I did it. I threw my jewelry box to the ground, making sure that the money wasn't entangled in silver and gold chains. How could I let this happen? I was never this careless. I was always on my shit, I always made sure, I always -

"Kayla Nicole, what the *FUCK* is going on?!" My mother screamed, pushing herself through the door I just barricaded.

"I lost my fucking money, just get out," I replied through gritted teeth, pushing Jordan aside to look through the clothes myself. "I fucking got it." I never cursed in front of my mother, ever. Even 'damn' was going too far, but today was different. Something changed today and I couldn't hold it back anymore.

She laughed, and it wasn't a 'haha, Kayla, you're so funny' laugh either. It was the kind where I knew I was in trouble, the kind of laugh she gives before she tries to beat my ass. It didn't frighten me today, however; today, it annoyed me. I wanted nothing to do with her outburst or her sarcastic ass attitude. She just needs to go lay the fuck down and sleep the day away like she's been doing. "Where the fuck is my money, Kayla?"

I scoffed. "First of all, it's *my* money. Second, I'm finding it. Leave me alone."

Jordan panicked in the background, pacing circles back and forth which only made the situation worse. He either had something to do with this jux, or he was just really, really nervous that his free ride in my apartment was over. "Just tell her the truth, babe." I looked over at him. The truth? He wanted us to come clean? He'd be homeless (according to him), I'd be in rehab and my family would disown me in a second. I looked over my mother's shoulder to him and he winked. "Tell her what's really been going on."

"Yeah, tell me what's really going on, Kayla." She was fucking seething and her anger made me worse. How dare she be mad right now? I was the one that got robbed, I was the one going through this shit the worst, not her. She wasn't going to be the one sick tomorrow, she wasn't going to be the one who lost two friends.

"Tell her about Brian and Christina, babe." What about them? I didn't understand, and then he winked again. "Tell them about it's really been their dope bags you've been hiding for them, tell her it was them who stole the money."

"I knew it," she sniffled "I fucking knew it. Why would you hang out with them?"

"I...I wanted friends..." I said quietly. Is this really fucking working? Is this going to be how I get away with this? I mean yeah, I blamed people all the time, but was she really, fully, 100% believing me? Why am I not coming up with such perfect lies lately? Damn.

"I don't think you realize, but I bring my lockbox to work with me every day because I'm scared, Kayla. I'm scared of the people you bring home. I'm scared that I'm going to come home and find you dead by even just experimenting once." She was sobbing now, and I was too. I didn't mean to make her scared in her own home; it was true, too. She was bringing her lockbox with her methadone to work with her every day. That hurt me a lot. "No matter what, you are my baby girl and I love you. 17 or not, adult or not, you are my baby. Please Kayla, please, please, please."

She was begging, and I was crying harder. Jordan was standing in the corner of my room, watching the whole scene unfold and not really saying much besides words of encouragement to us. 'It'll be okay', or 'it's over now' and corny shit like that.

Eventually, we all calmed down and went to the living room. My mother told me she'd give me more money to go shopping with BUT she'd hold it and would be checking receipts. Fine, whatever, I'd make it work.

Jordan was crying on the loveseat. "I can't believe they'd do this," he said between sobs. "Brian was my best friend. They made fun of my singing. They laughed at me." Apparently, before they left, Christina and Taylor laughed at him; they said that his voice was 'too high and girly'. It was, seeing as his inspiration was Vic Fuentes. The whole apartment building heard him when he sang.

He was still sobbing and I just couldn't take it. "Do you want me to come at them again?" He shook his head no. They already blocked our numbers and blocked us on Facebook, but I'd still try to find a way. "Do you want tooooo....eat?" It was like dealing with a fucking child because again, he shook his head no.

"Do you want an ice pop?" My mom burst out laughing as he shook his head yes, but that only made him cry more. I gave her an evil eye as I held my own laughter back. "She's not laughing at you, just the fact this is happening, that's all."

"Oh yeah, that's it." She said sarcastically, going to the kitchen for an ice pop.

How did my life get like this? I was dating a fucking idiot, I just got robbed for 120$ by two 'friends', and I was a 17 year old heroin addict. Where did I ever go wrong?

Chapter Eight

Somehow, we found a new dealer. An older African American guy named LB, and when he talked his fat body jiggled. He only sold double-sealed 'philly' bags, known for being blue and being stamped with the Batman symbol - that's how you knew they were LB's. They were 10$ and although sometimes they were good, they were almost always as bad. Anytime we copped from him in the Dollar General parking lot, I prayed they'd be a good batch.

I hated him, he scared the fuck out of me. One time I had to meet him on my own. I hiked myself up the SUV's passenger door and got in, doing the exchange and making small talk.

"So what you like to do?" He asked, locking the door.

What do I like to do? I don't know, do heroin..that's why I'm here, fucking idiot. "Uhm...I dunno, hang out?"

He smiled, the spots on his face moving places. "Oh damn...aight...I see you..hanging out, that's wassup. Ya man know?"

I nodded my head. "Uhm, yeah...he knows…"

"Ima give you a call later girl," he smirked, unlocking the doors. "Damn, I love a girl who can hang."

I got out and ran to my apartment. It wasn't until I told various friends the story, that I had just told my drug dealer I apparently prostitute myself. I threw up, and it wasn't because of the heroin.

I started to hang out with Scott again and I was really, really happy. No longer did I have to invite Jordan, but instead I went out to be a teenager and be free and he'd sit in my apartment, crying to my mother how he thought I was cheating on him. I never was, but in all honestly, I wanted to. I wanted to hurt him like he hurt me; I wanted him to suffer like I did.

So, I got a new group of friends. One of my old best friends from the summer, Angie, was dating a guy in one of the local bands around our area. He'd bring his drummer, this kid James who gave me all the attention in the world when I needed it. We'd go over to his house, pack Scott's car tight with people again and get drunk off hipster beer like Pabst's.

People liked being around me again and Scott thought I was sober. In fact, whenever I needed to get my 'medicine' (my dope, but I told him it was suboxone) he'd take me. I was working at Chic-Fil-A so I was starting to bring in some money again. He'd take me to this kid Justin; Justin was a tall, chunky white kid I had known since I was 14 via David. He was selling dope (and doing it, too) and usually delivered, but when he couldn't Scott took me to him because he didn't want me to be sick.

He took me all the way out to Stuyvesant and Rutherford, too and that was great...until when we were leaving a guy jumped on his car to get our attention. He said he didn't want me to be sick, but he'd never bring me back. To this day I laugh about it.

Most days ended up in me going to work with Scott picking me up, then we'd go out and run the town like we used to. The only difference these days was that I was doing heroin, but they never knew. They thought I was clean, and I was never going to let them on to that dark side of my life. I was secretive, and they never knew because I was outgoing. I was a heroin addict, but they never knew because they didn't have a basic concept of withdrawal. They thought I'd still be going through withdrawals, even though I was apparently clean since October. I'd keep my secret to the grave.

I was kind of talking to James, too; this cute tattooed kid from Princeton that had more money than I could ever hope to make in a year. He gave me attention and I loved it, reeling it in whenever he looked at me. He even lent me some money once, too - 10$ over what he said because he was drunk and didn't want to make change. He thought I was interesting, I guess - or maybe just pretty and wanted to fuck even though I never let him.

That was one thing I can say - I never, in my whole fucking life, sold myself for drugs. Never. I never took a naked picture, I never kissed anyone and never fucked anyone. I never begged, either. I got my money myself, even if I robbed someone it was more honorable than selling my body.

I got a lot of offers, too - and not just from LB. I had chances to work at the strip club across the bridge, or get a sugar daddy via a lonely guy I met on Facebook..but I never did it. I could never do it, I never even casually hooked up with people at parties. I loved attention, yes, and maybe more from guys when I was younger because of 'daddy issues', but I never went the full length. I valued myself more.

So when Viktoriya came into my life, I was stunned. She was this beautiful Russian and Italian girl I had met a few years ago, but she quickly became my best friend so quick, immediately bonding over the same heritage. Jess was gone, locked up over some stupid grand theft charge and Viktoriya scooped me into her skinny, pale arms. I loved her more than anything.

She made sure I was never sick, whenever she could. She made one of her boyfriend's drive all the way from Brooklyn, New York to my apartment so she could get high with me. Before she walked in my doors, she went over this guy's house..Ray? I'll call him Ray because my memory is shot now. She went over to Ray's house, did some shit with him with not a single care in the world, and came with a bundle. We cuddled all night, her little long-haired Chihuahua I had to sneak in the house between our legs.

I talked to her day and night, telling her my deepest secrets while she told me hers. We spoke Russian together, making jokes about people we hated behind their backs. She moved around a lot, but that never changed anything. She shared my dislike for Marie and David, she loved my snark and sarcasm and I loved her care for everyone. She was my whole heart.

She moved a lot, though, so I was left lonely even when I was around people. Nobody understood me, no matter how hard their facade was. I hated them. I hated the people who found out I was doing dope and apparently they were dope heads too because they tried a bump from their brother's aunt's dog or some shit. I hated people who lied and said they did dope because chances were, they never did it.

One time, Jordan and I were at this kid Chris's house. Chris had been my friend since I was 12, and Jordan's for about the same. He was really into backyard wrestling...until he did a bad trip and became a paraplegic. So here we are in his house, I'm dope sick as fuck and strumming chords on an acoustic guitar to take the time away - all my songs were about how dope sick I was because Pat and his friend Sean knew. Out of nowhere, this fucking loser Sean goes on a rant. A huge rant how I shouldn't do heroin because he recovered from this disease and his life is great just look at him, I should think more like him!

I spit in his face. "You're a fucking loser, and you never did heroin. You don't know what I feel like. You don't know how I fucking live. Fuck you. I should knock your dumb ass the fuck out right now, but for some reason Pat likes you." My anger was worse when I was dope sick.

I hated how people lied. Why would they lie about a lifestyle that no one wants? I didn't choose this. I didn't choose to become addicted to dope, it started off as just a one time thing.

And then it hit me. No one chooses to become an addict. It truly is a disease. My parents were addicts, their parents, and even *their* parents were addicts; there was no hope for me. I wasn't strong enough to 'break the cycle' like I had always thought.

I got this girl Stacy who was there and I fucked with to drive us home, and as soon as I walked into the door I cried, apologizing to my mother for all the shit I've ever talked in my life about drug addicts.

My life was falling apart, and everyone and their mothers could see it.

I went to Florida to visit my family in the middle of April. I needed a break, I needed to get the fuck away. I robbed someone for 12 subs (suboxone) and was going to bring them on the plane so I wouldn't be sick the whole time I was there. I divided them equally: Our ride got 4 for the ride, so that meant Jordan would get 4 and I'd get 4. In theory, it was a perfect idea. I had only maybe two weeks to go, and there was no way I'd run out before then.

But like all addicts, I don't know my limits; I do not know how to handle things in the correct manner. I did one of them before work at Chic-Fil-A and felt great; my body felt normal, like I had never done drugs a day in my life. I moved like a dancer through the fast food restaurant, ringing up customers and bagging orders so quick the managers were in awe with me. I guess it was because I took it at the right time the night before, but I was perfect and felt like I could live this way forever.

And then I got money and did some dope. Before I knew it, the subs were gone and I was leaving at 5:00 P.M to Newark Airport for my flight to Orlando. I cried the whole ride, making some bullshit excuse that I just was going to be homesick. I didn't want to leave - I couldn't. I would die out there with no drugs in my blood. I would literally fucking die. I prayed at every red light we got stuck at for more, getting on the turnpike with knots in my famished stomach.

I could've missed it. By the time I got to the airport and found my way (and waited at every corner for Momom and Popop to walk faster), there was only ten minutes left until boarding is closed off. I don't know how I made it. I rushed through security, hurriedly taking my flats off and slamming the lighter that was in my pocket in a plastic bin. I got held up through the x-ray because of my pants (stupid black leggings with a little metal design) then trudged on, my luggage flopping away.

I made it. I stared at the entrance that led to the plane and contemplated for a long time. I could say I missed it; that it was Momoms fault, she's always late and Momom Taco Bell knew that. I wouldn't have to spend 11 days shitting my brains out and not being able to sleep, or having to wear a hoodie in the 87 degree weather because my body can't get comfortable. I could run away from this all and really, truly, 100% prepare.

But I didn't. I missed Momom and Popop Taco bell, Aunt Erica and Isabella (my cousin, but because I'll never have nieces or nephews I call her my niece), and I would even see my father. My fucking father. I haven't seen him or even really heard from him since he was supposed to send 80$ but bailed three weeks ago. I needed to see everyone. My heart was fucking lonely and hurt most of the time, and more than anything I wanted to be in a house where I didn't have to worry about how I'd eat next and where my next meal came from. I'd have sloppy hugs from Isabella and bond with my Aunt Erica. I'd have time to be happy - even if going through severe withdrawal.

So I went. I got on that fucking Jetblue plane and went. The three hours went quickly thanks to *Love And Hip-Hop New York,* the anxiety gone via a bundle of dope that I did when I went into the airport bathroom. This was it. I couldn't go back now. I had to do this like a big girl.

I arrived late and as always they greeted me as soon as I got off the terminal; Momom and Popop Taco Bell with their big smiles, my dad with his crooked grin. I loved them. I made the right decision. I was so happy.

It was 9 PM by the time I got to their house in The Villages, Florida. They had a house built because they were in one of the newer communities and it was more beautiful from the last time I saw them. It was the kind of house that you felt small in, and it wasn't because their TV was mounted on the living room wall, looming over you as you walked in. But even then it felt like home, and I finally felt like I'd be able to sleep in peace. I wouldn't have to run the streets anymore, I could finally enjoy being young.

I went to sleep last night with the air blasting and the TV on MTV - something I could never do at home. We didn't have cable, and even in the dead of summer the air couldn't always be on because we were too broke to afford the PSE&G bill. I was in bliss. I could even wake up and drink soda! Soda! The only times we had soda in my apartment was when my mother had an extra two dollars and could afford it at Dollar General. I didn't care about the withdrawals I would face. I would be happy.

Until the next day, when I woke up at 11:30 in the morning and threw up beside the bed. I hastily turned the air off, throwing on a hoodie and popping more Imodium than I should and crawled to the bathroom. Momom Taco Bell usually slept late, and because Popop Taco Bell was so into his black and white western cowboy films I was able to crawl past them. I didn't take into account that my father would even be awake, so when he was outside the bathroom door waiting for me with his tattooed arms crossed, I jumped out of my skin.

"What are you on?" He hissed, dragging me to my bedroom for the next week and a half. He lyed on my bed and began to flip through channels, waiting for my answer.

"N-nothing, why?" I stuttered. It figures the one parent that doesn't pay attention to me will call me out on my bullshit and insist I was getting high. It made me mad. Who the fuck does he even think he is? How dare he even pretend to care?

"You were complaining about restless leg last night, you almost shit yourself as soon as you woke up, and not to mention the throw up right here," he pointed his index finger to now stained beige carpeting "What is it? Klonopins? You tried offering me them to get me to send you that 80-"

"Which you never sent," I cut him off now, the anger dripping on my words. Ever since he quit methadone and his own Klonopin cold turkey, he had a holier than thou attitude going on about drugs. He was always like that with my mother, but now me? His own fucking blood? I forgot how much he got under my skin. "I thought it would help. I don't eat most of the time and I need money. I don't get high. I don't have enough money for anything."

And that was that. He was quiet again, just like when I was little and we'd sit in silence the whole car ride from Trenton to Staten Island. It was never an uncomfortable silence since I learned to deal with it, but it was annoying. I hadn't seen him in months and he had nothing to talk about with me; we had nothing in common. We liked the Mets, and Great Grandma Edith was our favorite person in the world - that was it. We looked like fucking twins but had no connection besides him being the winner to get my mom pregnant. It was ridiculous.

I was miserable all fucking day. It was reaching almost 90 degrees in The Villages, but I still had on a lightweight hoodie; I never sweat, and I was always freezing my ass off.

The highlight of my day was seeing my Aunt Erica during her break at lunch. Momom Taco Bell took us to a Japanese restaurant to meet her, and it was always the same tight-hugged greeting that it always ways. I was always better around her, always myself. It wasn't like hanging out with a strict aunt, but more of a best friend that would never leave me. To this day, she's the only person that makes sure to text me a couple times a week making sure I know she loves me.

Every single day fucking sucked. Jordan barely talked to me, and when he did he was nodding out in his house, lying his dumb ass off about it. David, of all people, talked to me more than him, even though it was only to wire him 50$ that he 'swears he'll pay back.' I refused my ass off. If I wasn't on the toilet, I was shivering under the covers and refusing to get out of my room. I had a cold I would say, and they wouldn't think twice. The Small family was infamous for getting sick, so why would this be any different?

I begged my Momom and Mommy to buy me a plane ticket home. I couldn't do it here. Anytime I went to the Town Square I'd run off, hitting my veins anytime I saw someone my age to signal them that I needed heroin. It never worked, and I only looked like a fucking idiot instead. I had so much money and I couldn't spend it on anything. I wanted to fucking kill myself. The whole 'going cold turkey' thing sucked. There was no benefit from it, I wanted nothing to do with being clean if this is what I had to do. I couldn't do it. I had to leave.

I loved being with my family, but my feelings felt like they were constantly invalidated. There were no pictures of me around the house, instead what felt like tens of thousands of Isabella were taking their place on the walls. A million thoughts constantly ran through my brain - was it because I refused to move down south with them? Or was it because they just liked Isabella more? Was it because of her mother, my Aunt Erica, was a better child than my father ever was, and in return, they didn't have to raise her like they did with me? If that was the case, that wasn't my fault. I didn't mean for that to happen. When I wasn't throwing up, I was crying - when I wasn't crying, I was begging God to kill me.

I stayed at my Aunt's apartment for 2 days. It was a pretty, kinda big complex with a playground smack dab in the middle that I knew Isabella must love going on. It was beautiful, and I was jealous that my grandparents paid for her to live there while they barely helped me. Besides that, I had fun with her. She cooked me dinner and we went on adventures throughout Florida. We slept in the same bed and watched scary movies like *Sinister* or *Flight* - that one really fucked me up, seeing as my flight was in 4 days.

4 days. I could do it. I could really, really fucking do it. I was starting to be able to sleep through the night now, the restless leg only bothering me a little bit. I was more social now and even went tanning at the pool. That was fun...until I got sunburnt. Have you ever been dope sick and sun burnt? It's not a life for anyone. I wouldn't wish it on my worst goddamn fucking enemies.

I would wake up around 11, eat breakfast, go out with my grandparents, come back home, sometimes go out to eat dinner, then watch TV until 3 in the fucking morning and ass out. It was a routine I built myself. I had to pass the time, and a routine would do just that. I could do it. I could fucking do this.

On the last night before I left for the plane, I was repacking all my clothes before going out to eat at the TGI Fridays. I was refolding every article of clothing I owned and bought on the trip here, and stumbled on a piece of paper. And not just any piece of paper, but a glassine bag. A dope bag. A tore in half, empty dope bag with a red stamp. I threw a fucking fit...only after I licked it clean, hoping for anything to make me feel better. If I could get away with just the glassine bag, maybe I could get away with an actual dope bag? Like, one filled with the powder? I contemplated that, making a mental note to try next time I came down here, then left for the restaurant.

Dinner went by so quick, and before I knew it I was hugging my aunt goodbye, sobbing along with her. I didn't want to be here anymore, but I would miss them. I hated living in the apartment. I never had food, I had no cable; I ran the streets every night robbing people for money so I wouldn't be dope sick. I didn't want to go back to that life. I wanted to stay here and be happy and be taken care of for once. I would eat every day, I would be able to get my license and GED and they'd even help me pay for cosmetology school at The Salon Professional Academy (not my first choice, but have you seen the commercials? Fucking hilarious.) I would have a life. I wouldn't be miserable. I would even soon be able to sleep normally. What was the point of going back?

Heroin. Heroin and taking care of a mother who couldn't take care of herself half of the time was the point.

So I hugged everyone goodbye, got back to the house, and stayed up until 4 A.M. We left the house, and I only looked back when I heard my dog that I had since I was 7 years old crying in the background.

I was so excited to go home, I couldn't sleep the whole time. Momom and Popop Taco Bell were taking the train with me, they were going to New Jersey to visit and it was easier to take the same flight. That made things a lot easier. My Popop's never ending smile made my scared-to-fly anxiety gone, and Momom Taco Bell falling asleep playing mahjong made me laugh. I wished so fucking bad I wasn't like this, that I could've actually enjoyed my 11 days with them instead of in pain every day. I wish this didn't happen.

The flight was over too soon, and meeting me outside the gate were my everyday Momom and Popop. As happy as I was to see them, to run into their arms, it hurt me to leave Momom and Popop Taco Bell. I didn't know when I would see them again, or even fucking talk to them.

I hugged them and kissed them goodbye, trying my hardest not to cry in front of them but God, it didn't matter. I cried a lot, and this time it was for an actual reason. I wanted so badly to apologize to them, to say I was sorry for complaining the whole time and to make sure they knew how much I loved them. But of course, that never happened. Instead, I said the usual 'bye' and 'I'll text and call you' and 'I love you so much', and left. Just like that.

I rushed to the car, the one Momom had to borrow from her mom because her 95' Malibu wouldn't make it. For the first time in 11 days, I fell asleep easy. I was home. I wouldn't be sick. I'd be fine soon.

I made it home, and Jordan was waiting for me with my mother. It was the happiest I had ever fucking been to see their faces. In between telling vacation stories and showing clothes I picked out, I made a call to my drug dealer. I needed 3 buns. The hour lasted so fucking long.

But then I got into routine again. I poured three bags out, snorted them, and the only difference was I got high. For the first time in 12 days I actually got high instead of doing bags just to get well. I was so happy I didn't even care that made a burn in my knuckle because I was finally *high*.

I'd call my Momom and Popop Taco Bell tomorrow, just to make sure they knew what an amazing time they had. I'd make sure they knew how much I loved them.

But tomorrow never came.

A few days after, Brian and his new girlfriend Brenda came back into our lives again. He apologized and I didn't really care anymore, I was just excited I didn't have to cop off of LB and could go back to getting 5$ bags. I also really, really got along with Brenda for the most part; she was too fragile to rob me, too innocent at that point. She'd only been doing dope for about a month, and also saw the way I came at her when she asked to split bags - she wouldn't risk getting even more of a rude ass reaction by robbing me. She wasn't as ballsy as Christina.

My habit picked up right where it left off. It was fun getting so high I puked because my tolerance went down, but after a few days, it was right back to where I started. I was sick for 12 days for nothing.

March/April 2013.

Chapter Nine

The months blurred into one constant haze. I wasn't ready for my birthday. I dreaded it every time I looked at the calendar. It was here. June 5th was finally here.

Scott picked me up early that day, then picked up Justin because he needed a ride to get the initial 'brick of the day'. He gave me extra and I thanked him, holding back crying until I finally snorted enough dope to make a grown man drop.

I was 18. I made it. I finally made it and had nothing to show for it.

The last almost year of my life was spent nodding out, fighting with my mother and boyfriend, and getting money from my Momom. I worked a shitty job maybe 25 hours a week, and all of that money went to bundles of heroin. I dropped out of high school, and instead of getting fitted for a cap and gown I was going to community service.

I looked into the mirror for a long, long time that day. I hated myself. I hated everything around me. I wasn't even getting high anymore, so what the fuck was the point of doing this shit anymore? Oh, so I wouldn't be sick..right.

Of all fucking people to come back into my life, Marie was that person. Scott picked me up one day and took me to the Morrisville river. It was such a beautiful night, and I remember looking over the river and wanting to change everything. The way Trenton's skyline danced over the waves, the way the beginning of summer's air hit my thighs; I could stay there forever.

"You know, Marie is sorry."

I laughed, raising my eyebrows. Scott had a tendency to believe anything a pretty girl said.

"No, really, she is." He began, trying to convince me. *"She's really, really sorry and just wants her friend back. Please give it a try."* He *just wanted to fuck and wanted me as 'his best friend' to be nice and to also have a friend in her.*

But for some reason, I believed him and we got close again. We did everything together again. She was clean because she was pregnant with her second child and when I was sick she'd rub my back and when she had morning sickness I'd rub her tummy. It was fucking disgusting. Our relationship was sick.

But today was my birthday, and today shit was different. I was going to have my first ever surprise party and I was so happy. I made sure to look so cute, too. I had this cute pink dress on, and my favorite wedges borrowed from my mother. My hair was in a bun but I had these really cute aviator's and said fuck my glasses. I couldn't wait.

Scott would be there, and James and Ally and Sarla and Stacy and all of James's band and people who actually liked me! Scott picked me up right as Angie texted me saying she couldn't make it. *They were really trying to fool me!* I picked up another bundle of a shit stamp called 'Mustang' and did six off the bat, wanting to be really high and not feeling shit from earlier.

"Alright, you ready?" Scott asked after picking Marie up.

"Uhm yes!" I beamed. "Of course!"

We pulled up to this kid Dom's house and at first, I was confused, but then brushed it off. I was friends with Dom and had been to parties at his house before, so maybe they were just using his house for that.

I hopped out of the car and walked the perfect fucking model walk to the front step, taking my hair out of the bun so I'd have the perfect waves. No one would look better than me. Everyone would stare and it would be a good stare.

I opened the door, and no one was there. Confused, I treaded to Dom's room because maybe they were hiding out in different spots.

But they weren't. Instead, Dom had a little group of friends over and they were fucking playing Yu-Gi-Oh! Even Scott had joined them.

I looked at Marie, who's eye were filled with genuine sadness. "I didn't know, Kayla. I'm so sorry."

They all bailed out on me. Every single fucking one. Jordan wasn't even here with me, he was at some fucking girl's house and Jame's didn't even know it was my birthday. Viktoriya was MIA, Jess was locked up, and none of my friends even got an 'invite' apparently.

Everyone had forgotten about me. My dad didn't even text me.

Suddenly, I was alone again and running out of Dom's house to avoid their stares. Why were my birthday's always like this? I spent my 17th birthday waitressing and hanging out with just Scott in Quick Chek's parking lot, and I spent my 16th birthday drunk and crying because that's the night David and Marie 'fell in love'. This birthday was no better. I lost my insurance. I didn't have friends. I wasn't even fucking high.

The world was spinning around me. I couldn't breathe and had to lean myself against Scott's car to support myself, throw up threatening to spew out. I don't get it. I thought they were my friends again; I thought we were all best friends. Why? Why? Why, why, why?

Life sucks, and then you die, right? I was never that lucky.

My mother wasn't there when I got home, her late hours kept her at work until midnight but I stayed up waiting just to sit with her. I don't know where Jordan was and honestly, I didn't care. I was already lonely, he'd just add on to that.

Did I deserve this? Maybe this is what I got for robbing that guy in the hospital or stealing money out of that girl's purse at Chic-Fil-A. Maybe I deserved this for robbing Brian, for telling him that the suboxones that I traded for dope would make him feel better when in reality they were just pain meds my cat had gotten for getting fixed. Maybe they hated me all along, and they planned this out. This is what they had set, this is how they'd get me real good.

I hated my life. I did more dope and prayed to God to kill me in my sleep. I didn't want to do this shit anymore.

My birthday. June 5th, 2013.

Chapter Ten

Jordan had a bad habit inviting friends to sleep over without mine or my mother's permission. He felt like he owned my apartment, running around shirtless and eating all the food while not ever holding a job or giving my mother money. He just felt comfortable enough, somehow, to tell people it was *his new spot,* and to come over and chill.

It started off with Brian, and then his dope head friend Jake. Jake and Jordan had been best friends for years, in fact, one of the times I met Jordan when I was still dating David, his friend Jake was with him. Jake was known around the towns that made up Mercer County as a dope head. He was known to rob and lie and then fuck your girlfriend because, well, he was just that scummy. But here he was, inside my apartment doing dope with us because he had a connect and his parents kicked him out for stealing an iPad.

Jake was there for 2 days before he got annoying. I hated coming home from my dumb ass fast food restaurant job to find him nodding out on the porch. I would barely make it out of Momom's car and he was already asking for cigarettes. I'd yell no and lock myself in my room or even in the closet, smoking cigarettes no one knew I had. I was a fucking prisoner in my own house, and because I didn't want anything to happen between Jordan and me, I let it happen.

Anytime he would go get *my* dope with Jordan, they wouldn't ask how we were splitting up. If we only had 3, they'd only give me one and do one each for themselves, snorting it in my kitchen while my mother was in the other room. *Writing this now, I'm getting so mad and wish Jake* didn't block me on Facebook because I'd love to punch his dumb ass face.* His smelly ass would just smirk, then say some lame thing about how that's the game.

And then, about four days into his stay, there was a knock on my door. Obviously, it was David, fresh off his latest 2 month bid. I was *excited*, like the fucking idiot I was. My best friend/person I would marry would SURELY help me. He would never let Jordan and Jake be fucking losers and mooch everything off me. Only David himself was allowed to treat me like shit, after all.

But life doesn't work like that. Not for junkies, anyway. I would get into fights with Jordan, have to give all my cigarettes to Jake, and get mentally abused by David. I put up with Jake because of Jordan, and I put up with David because he held being a heroin addict over my head. His biggest threat was fucking me up and *then* telling my 'fat ass mother' I was a junkie. I just said okay and sorry, vehemently promising I wouldn't be annoying or needy or whatever I was being at that fucking moment. It was clear I would never win, and I had to take it and live with it. Jake only left after stealing 10$ from David and getting Jordan beat up for it.

Towards the end of June was my Uncle Shawn's wedding. The day was already going to shit because I had run out of dope and had to split a fucking 7$ bag with Jordan. He was never fucking sick, or just didn't get as sick as I did, and definitely didn't need it, but that was life. We made a commitment to go to this wedding and I just wasn't taking being sick as an excuse.

"I don't even wanna go to this bullshit," Jordan mumbled, fixing the collar to his 3$ dollar sports material shirt that his mother bought at Ross.

"You have to come, Jordan. What the fuck do you expect me to do right now?" David was in the room, watching bad Trenton graffiti videos while Jordan and I hurried to get dressed. He didn't care my ex boyfriend was in the same room, and maybe that should've been a sign for me to leave this sick relationship.

But it wasn't. So instead I tugged my white dress over my head and started to put my wedges on. "Like, really. What, you want David to fucking come? David, you wanna fucking come?"

David's head shot up. "I mean, I guess so."

"Oh, thank god. Thank you, dude." Jordan relaxed automatically, tossing his beat up Volcom's to the side of my room.

I rolled my eyes. "Whatever. This is gonna be fun to explain."

"Kay, I can't go," he replied sheepishly. "I have nothing to wear."

When it came to outward appearances, David was always on top of his. He would've never even *thought* about going to Ross's for a dress shirt. It would've been Polo and True Religion to the nines, which would've been a lot fucking nicer than Jordan's second hand embarrassment outfit. I felt bad. He genuinely embarrassed, and that kind of broke my heart.

Jordan sighed, picking up his shoes and putting them on.

"I'm sorry you have to go through this," I snapped. "Aw man, a night of free food and free booze for your bum ass. What a horrible night."

"Oh my god, Kayla." David laughed out, not expecting an outburst. "Calm down."

"No, no dude it's fine." Jordan rolled his eyes and picked up his iPod touch, going out to the porch to listen to screamo bands before Momom came.

I said goodbye to David, who begged me to come back quick because he had nothing to do. I made a promise of 7, knowing it wouldn't come true. I knew the wedding would be awkward, because, well, these people are fucking strangers. But anytime out from my heroin filled apartment was time I wanted. I'd treasure every awkward second of it.

Momom came a little while later, purple 95 Malibu coming around the corner like a chariot. Popop looked his best and Momom did too, shit, she even had me put in earrings for her. This wasn't just any ordinary event, no. Popop's only son was getting married. We'd have to hold our shit together for at least a few hours.

So we did, for a little bit anyway. Jordan and I started to get along and were on disposable camera duty for Momom. They even let me get in some formal pictures right before the ceremony, which to this day was one of the most perfect things in the world. I have it on my bucket list to look like my Uncle's wife on my own wedding day.

We had a few Klonopin, someone gave them to us for my bad anxiety and they went up our noses during the break between the reception.

"I'll never get married," I stated simply, wiping any residue of my nose.

"Oh, stop." Jordan said, his skinny legs walking around the Holiday Inn lobby.

Me, Momom, Laura, Uncle Shawn, Popop.

Same as above.

I was really JUST blinking and not nodding out. I swear.

At that point, the ideal answer from him would've been 'Oh, stop. We're gonna get married.' But it wasn't. His sentence stopped just as quickly as my heart had. Sure, I never had any images of him in a tux saying 'I do', but he was supposed to ride this out with me. He was supposed to get clean with me and we were supposed to have little tan skinned babies running around. We'd get a tiny ass apartment in Morrisville and be okay. We wouldn't hate each other as much as we did and my dad would walk me down the aisle and Jordan would love every moment of it a little bit more than I did so my heart never hurt.

But that wasn't his idea, it was mine. So I ended the subject and walked to the reception area, hoping the Klonopins would react with the half bag of dope and I'd feel a little bit better.

The rest of the night went slowly. Momom wouldn't let Jordan or I drink, I was sick as fuck, and I didn't know anyone; the DJ even skipped our table when he would interact with the crowd. David was texting me off the hook to come home because he was bored, my anxiety was through the roof, and I hated everyone.

After some convincing Momom took us home. I walked into my apartment door and was met with David screaming his head off.

"I'm sorry," I sighed, taking my wedges off. "It wasn't my fault."

"It really wasn't, bro. Momom just wanted to stay." Jordan intervened.

"I don't give a fuck. It's unacceptable. The only room I get wifi in this shit place is this room so for fucking 6 hours I was stuck here. It's not okay." He was pacing circles now, something his anger led him to. I wasn't in the mood for any of it.

The next morning I woke up to yelling, not like that was anything new. I walked to the bathroom to see David sitting on the toilet with a needle in hand, pointing a crooked finger to the tiled floor.

"Find my fucking needle, bitch!" David screamed to Jordan, who was now on the ground scouring.

"I am dude, I am!"

I rolled my eyes and walked to the living room to see my mom gone. I sat on the couch and pulled my fleece blanket over my body, lighting a cigarette and already hating the taste. My stomach was turning in knots and my nose had already started to snot everywhere. I looked at the clock. 1:18 P.M. Momom should be over soon with money, seeing as she got paid today. Today should be easy.

Jordan eventually found the needle head and attached it back to David's rig, helping him shoot up some scrapes he had. He ran out of the door after that, giving me a quick peck on the head and an excuse of his mom out front.

David started up shortly after that, as per usual.

"Hey Kayla, when are you gonna tell your mom you're a junkie?"
"Hey Kayla, when is your fat fuck mom gonna get a house?"
"Hey Kayla, do you wanna know why I fucked Marie when you went to Staten Island?"

I rolled my eyes each time, replying with a 'no' or a 'leave me alone'. He didn't ever like that.

"Don't be a fucking cunt because you're dope sick," he spat, putting his phone on the charger. "I'll call your mother in a fucking second and tell her what's good."

He went to the kitchen, leaving his phone on the table. And then it hit me.

I quickly snatched it in my hands, going into his contacts and beginning to search 'L' for Laura. He couldn't call my mother if he didn't have her number right?

I heard him singing, some bullshit song I didn't really care about before his phone shut off in my hand. *Fuck.* I forgot his phone was doing that now. If it was off when he got back, I'd be fucked. If he even found out I was on his phone, I'd really be fucked.

His phone started up again, and into his contacts I went again. L. Laura. It wasn't there, so I started to type in 'K' - his phone shut off again. *Fuck, fuck fuck fuck.* I peeked my head into the long hallway of my apartment that lead into the kitchen. He was still in there, but my time was running out. I had to end this two week long abuse before I lost my mind.

His phone started up again, and I repeated my process. Contacts. K. Kayla's mom.

It was there. In all of its fucking glory, it was there.

I held the button down, sweat dripping off my forehead as I prayed for the phone to not shut off. I heard his footsteps coming down the hallway, the heavy *clunk* of Nike meeting fake hardwood. My heart was making the same noise.

"Kayla, I ate the-"

It deleted. It fucking deleted. Oh my god. I was free.

"I don't care." I snapped, a smirk on my face. I was free. I could get him out of my house, he would never call my mother. He wouldn't be able to.

"Excuse me?" A blonde eyebrow raised up. *Free.*

"I said, I don't care." *Free at last.*

"Don't come at me because you're dope sick, you got that? I'm the only one fucking helping you around this shit hole."

"I'm not sick." I was still smirking through my lie. 2:00 P.M. She'll be here soon. I won't be sick. *Free.*

He didn't like that because my face was met with a plastic green cup. "Knock it the fuck off, Kayla!"

"What are you gonna do, hit me?"

The air changed in the apartment, and I knew I had done it. I blew the fuse, and there was no coming back. This was it, this was the blowout.

He jumped over the table, all 5'4 of him crashing on top of me as his hands held my shoulders down. "What the fuck did you just say?"

"What are you gonna do, huh? You gonna fucking hit me? I'm not Marie, I don't give a fuck." I maneuvered my way from under him, making my way towards the hallway.

Free at last. I was free.

It happened quickly then.

A fist met with the bone below my eye, and I was yelling 'get off of me' before I could even comprehend what was happening. He pinned me against the wall, with one forearm pinning my neck and the other hand just about to collide with my face.

My front door opened, and it wasn't my mother. It wasn't even Jordan. It was my neighbors, all 8 of them.

"Is he hittin' you, ma?!" One of them yelled.

I simply nodded my head.

"Oh, hell nah bitch!"

The two males tackled him, and then all the females came running after. They got his body on the couch and cornered him into the corner, all of them connecting blow after blow. One of them hugged me and wiped the tears off my face while the other got his shit out of my apartment.

They chased him out of the building, calling him names while he called his sister to pick him up.

I was free at last.

His sister came and tried to talk shit, angry that her brother had gotten jumped but stopped when she saw my busted face. I didn't care, I just simply handed her his shit and left.

Brian and Brenda came over right after, freaking out when they saw my face and heard what happened. Momom didn't come until 5 PM, and that was only after I told her what had happened. Jordan showed up, too, but not because he truly cared I just got beat up. He held no intention of finding David and making sure no one ever harmed his girlfriend because in his head he was only here for the heroin. His purpose was already fulfilled.

I called Marie and told her what happened. Her response was like a typical best friend, but she was holding back something. I ignored it and hung up, convinced that it was all in my head. David was gone, I was free. Nothing could ever possibly bother me again.

A few days later I got off from my shift at Chic-Fil-A not expecting anything different to happen, the only weird thing was that Jordan's mother came into my job and asked where he was and why he wasn't answering his phone. She thought he was doing heroin, and she needed to know the truth.

I don't know how she ever found out. Maybe it was because he robbed his cousin for 120$? Actually...it was definitely because of that.

Anyway, Momom brought me home that night and Jordan was waiting with dope in his hand. He told me about how his mom came to visit because she was scared he was getting high, and right as I was about to do my bag he dropped the world on top of my shoulders.

"She's sending me to rehab. I'll be gone next Thursday at 11 A.M."

I did my bag, then reacted...horribly. "But...why? You can't go..you can't just leave."

We had our problems, but some nights weren't so bad. Some nights I really, really loved him; some nights we spent all night talking to each other or just hanging out or just laid next to each other and read. We had inside jokes and we had fun and we had pictures for Facebook...it wasn't always bad, right? Or was it, and I'm only thinking like this because he's leaving and my heart literally cannot take anyone else leaving?

Maybe.

"I know Kayla, I know. I tried to fight her and convince her I was fine but I'm only gonna be there for a month. I'll be out for my 21st birthday and nothing will change." He tried his best to convince me, he really did. He tried to calm my shaking body as best as he could, but nothing he said or did worked. I was already gone.

We were together at that point for a year - my longest relationship since David. I had begun this fucked up drug journey with him! Because of him, even! He couldn't just leave, not after everything we went through..he owed me that. He owed me to stay, and he'd just leave like my father? Like my mother when I was a child?

"I promise you, it'll be okay." He kissed me on the forehead, then began to do his dope on the couch. These days he was smoking it because it apparently gave him the same feeling as shooting it. Whatever. I wasn't ready for any of it. I didn't want to be alone, I didn't want to face this world by myself, I had done that enough and hated it. It made me into something I could hardly stand.

I must've begged him every day of the week to not go, to tell his mother to fuck herself. He wouldn't listen.

'She won't let me not go', he'd say. 'I have to.'

But he didn't have to - he didn't even want to go. But he was a 20 year old boy and depended on people to give him shit because he never worked a day in his life, so he listened to what mommy said. I couldn't stand it.

I'd go to work and he'd be home, smoking all of my cigarettes and doing more dope than he should. He'd tell me it's only fair because I wasn't giving him half of the bundle anymore and he needed to get it out of his system before rehab. I told him it wasn't fair because I worked almost every day and he didn't; I made money and that money bought this bundle of dope, therefore I should get more. We fought almost every day.

My mother knew something was going on and cried with me, too. She didn't like to see her only child crying on the bathroom floor, not wanting to even live. She also didn't understand the big deal, she thought he was going to his grandmother's in North Carolina to visit. She thought I'd still talk to him every day. She didn't know.

The day finally came. I set up a ride to take me to Stuyvesant to cop early - Dom and Sarla. They took me around 11, the dealer accidentally handed Dom the dope instead of me, and that was okay. They understood and weren't mad at me - I'd been sober for awhile, and this was very heartbreaking after all. They would even make sure to pick me up later and hang out with me so I wouldn't be upset.

My mother cried the whole time we were saying our goodbyes. Story goes that we apparently got into a fight, but I don't remember that. I just remember him wanting some dope and me saying no. He was leaving, I needed it. He'd be in rehab and be force fed suboxone, he'd be fine.

I looked at him for awhile that day. He looked the same to me from the first day we met on Scott's porch. Skinny body, flippy hair, even the same fucked up half-missing braces. For a year of my life, he occupied my world completely and it wasn't the same for him. I fought girls for him - innocent girls that did nothing, he just wanted to see how high I'd go and I always went; he didn't do the same, letting me get beat up by David because he didn't want to deal with his mouth.

"Well, call me as much as you can." I don't know why, but I was sobbing at this point. I guess I always cried, but this was more of a pathetic, my life is over sob.

I don't remember what really happened after that, just that I ran after him in the rain yelling to him, not *at* him. I just needed him to know that I loved him and that I would wait no matter what. I wouldn't get clean because that was just silly, but I'd wait every fucking day for him.

The only good part about all of this was that Viktoriya moved back to Trenton. She spent the weekend with me as my mom couldn't and held me the whole time, making sure to kiss my forehead and cuddle me until I knew she wouldn't leave my side like everyone else.

Brian and Brenda were there, too. Brian was my best friend in the whole entire world, assuring me that Jordan did miss me and that everything would be the same, no matter what.

And then I made the fatal mistake of checking his Facebook messages, a place that had been proven deadly but for some reason I had to. I had to know if he was really in rehab, I had to know if he was just hiding, I had to know if…

My heart stopped. A message to this girl Kaitlyn. With shaky fingers I clicked on her picture, knowing the worst was coming but fervently hoping for the best case situation. I dropped my phone to the ground, Viktoriya putting her long arms around me.

He was with her the night before he left. He kissed her and sang to her; he sang her a song he wrote just for her. I read the lyrics and screamed. This was a song he wrote for our baby that miscarried, right in front of me.

"Why? Why why why why" I moaned out, burying my head in Viki's chest.

"Oh, baby, I don't know," she crooned to me while petting my hair. "Baby, I'm so sorry. Just cry, it's okay. Just cry."

And that's what I did until the next day when Brian and Brenda came over...then I cried some more, did some dope, and was angry. I was going through the grieving process quick, the best help being a bundle with a bright neon green stamp titled 'Swine Flu'. I nodded out in between crying sessions, trying to make my point across that I'd knock him the fuck out but never making it.

I was hypocritical, and I didn't give a fuck. No one else was allowed to deal with his shit but me. No one else was allowed to get high with him or make him rice with soy sauce and scrambled eggs but me. No one was allowed to hate him but *me*.

That day via Viki's phone with Brenda in the back nodding out while spying on Jordan's Facebook.

I quit my job at Chic-Fil-A, got one at a pizza place, then never went back and got a job with Brian and Brenda going door-to-door and asking if people wanted renovations or new roofs. I made 10$ an hour and was kind of proud about that, besides the fact I worked with a racist and sexist piece of shit. I got a really shitty shoulder tattoo by Chris the paraplegic (I literally laugh about that all the fucking time), nodded out on some dope called 'White House' that almost killed me; all the while Chris's girlfriend filmed a guy shoving his tongue down my throat while I was in and out of consciousness, barely able to say no. I was out of control. I had more heroin to do for myself and that was really, really bad. My habit became twenty times worse and I was fucking greedy. No longer were the days that Brian was mooching 4 bags out of me because now I got *sick*. My dope sickness evolved from backaches and the wind hurting my skin to vomiting and shitting at the same time, all the while I had cold sweats and didn't even have enough strength to wipe my face. I needed every ounce I could get.

My mother was constantly finding my empty bags and I'd blame them on Jordan. I told her the 'truth' - he started using when David lived with us for that week and his mother sent him to rehab. I kept the empties incase he came back and wanted them because *I loved him oh so much*. She believed me and ignored her gut feeling; I was getting sloppy and we both knew it.

Scott and Angie and James and literally everyone else stopped talking to me because - surprise! - Marie had told them all I was doing dope and taking it into their cars. While that was true, it was only to sabotage my fucking life because she got off on that. She got off on making me lonely and miserable. That's why her voice sounded weird the day David beat me up, that's why she cut our conversation short. It pissed her off that he was even in my house, fuck beating me up because that meant nothing to her.

I was alone. The world was fucking against me, and the only friends I had were three heroin addicts and my upstairs neighbor, Laura, and her three daughters. Laura was the only one to look me in my face, her long fake talons touching the side of my face, and said to get help. She fed me when my mother and I had no food, she made sure she told me she loved me when no one else did. I was always still so alone.

My PTSD was bad. Sometimes I forgot I was 18, instead my mind tricking me into being 8 again. I was always depressed, and every god damn night I begged God to kill me. I didn't want to live this way every day, but I wasn't ready for help. I was fucking stuck.

Chapter Eleven

I started to do normal teenage things with anyone that would give me the time. I went to the beach, I went to the movies, I got tattoo's and flirted with guys that I had no intentions of doing things with. I got drunk with my neighbors and smoked blunts, I even would walk with Laura to the high school to watch her daughters play field hockey.

Brian and Brenda were my only everyday life lines. We even had jokes.

"Yo, the other day when I was waiting for D this car pulled up to me, right? And I'm just standing and he goes, 'hey girl, where's yo daddy?' so I'm freaked the fuck out already, because like what the fuck, so I go 'uhm...at home…' and he looks at me like I'm fucking nuts and goes 'nah, ya REAL daddy.' So it just happens at that time D walked out of his house and I pointed to him and ran away."

Brian and Brenda both laughed, repeating 'Hey Kayla, where's yo real daddy' a thousand times.

July turned to August, then to September and all of the sudden it was October and I had heard only once from Jordan. He called me one night I was at Momom's getting money and I was happy...until my phone died. I didn't see him until he came to my house one day. We reconciled, made up, and he stayed at my apartment again for a few weeks.

When I was in the 5th grade, I got my first name plate for graduating. It was beautiful, expensive, and it took Momom Taco bell and I took days to pick the perfect one out. A silver with gold background, double plated diamond beauty. I remember in 6th grade I got made fun of for it until I pointed out the 14k stamp on the back, then they thought it was cool. It was my prized possession and anyone in this memoir will tell you that. The only time I took it off was when I was dying my hair, besides that it never left my neck.

Showers, fights, even when I had my appendix on they somehow allowed it. It was my fucking pride and joy, my trademark even. I was never seen without it.

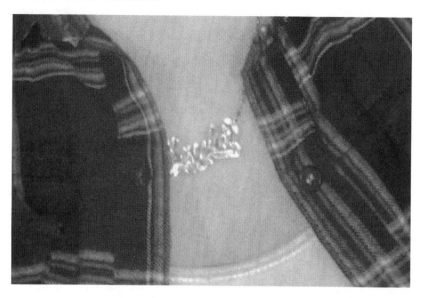

So when I was sick and lying on the couch unable to get money and my hands reached up to take my necklace off, I was stunned. I had no fucking control over myself. I went to the bathroom and took it off, making sure it was still as beautiful as ever. *Of course it was.*

I called the only person who would take me to pawn it -David. In reality, I should've just called Brian and been done, accepting the 4 bag loss but I was stubborn and wanted everything I could get. Besides, I was already sick and needed dope and David would give me a bag he saved from last night. The Grudge was the stamp and apparently it was double sealed. I was excited.

They picked me up, and with shaking hands I walked into the Check Cashing & Gold buyers place on South Broad St. I handed the Spanish kid who worked at the counter my necklace, slipping it under the bullet proof glass they had making a wall between him and I. Justin hurriedly gave him his ID, not even giving me a chance to get mine out. He knew he'd get a bag out of this, too. I wish I went with Brian.

"120." That was it. I had just sold my prized possession for 120$.

Justin had his girlfriend drop us off in the middle of Trenton since she refused to take us to cop. She didn't wanna help us die, something like that. I thought it was funny coming from the girl who tattooed a literal dick squirting cum behind her ear, but I shut my mouth. Whatever, I didn't mind walking, which was a good thing because we did a lot of it. We were in Chambersburg, passed Momom's house, then ended up on disgusting ass Jersey St. We went to a dealer named Kay, some guy they always cop off, but he only had 10$ bags and they didn't want me to spend my money on a 100$ bun even though they were 'Camden bags', so off we went.

Right away someone came up to us, saying a bun was 60$. Justin said yes right away without asking anybody first, without even realizing that was 20$ above usual. So he handed the dude the money and we waited down the block, every second that went by more sketch.

"I got bricks for 200 if ya'll want some good shit," someone called out to us. "But ya'll junkies always waste ya money."

"We're good," David answered back hostile as fuck. "I get bricks for 120$."

"Then it's shit, and your cops." By this time Justin was walking towards the dude he gave the money too. He looked in the tissue paper he got and bugged.

"Where the fuck is my shit?" Justin screamed.

"You got 30 seconds to get the fuck off my block," the random dude threatened "Or ya'll dead."

It was just like that. That fucking simple. I didn't think I looked like a cop, either. Laura had braided the side of my head to make it look like I had an undercut, and I was wearing an Adidas track pants and a fucking jacket from Dots. I was obviously sick as fuck too if he couldn't tell by the massive amount of snot dripping out of my nose.

Justin wouldn't move. In fact, as pussy as he can be, he was the first one who tried to fight. Three dudes surrounded him and smashed a bottle of Henny on the ground, then with the remaining pieces threw it at his head.

"David please, please let's go. Please stop, Justin, please." I begged and fucking begged. I was never a pussy, ever. In fact, I always tried fighting; tonight was not one of those nights. "Please, we have to go."

David was fine with it, considering Justin a lost cause up until he heard his heavy body fall to the ground and heard them hitting him. "We gotta help."

He ran toward the group, and I ran after him. And then it kind of just happened.

I don't know how, but somehow the two of us ended up on the ground right next to Justin. Just like that, we were surrounded by a group of 4 men getting jumped. We all got pistol whipped, and only after that were we free to leave.

"If I ever see any of ya'll dumb ass crackers again, it's ya head."

We walked to Kay's house and had no choice: with the rest of my money (50 fucking dollars), I got 5 Camden bags. One to Justin, and one to David which left me with two to myself. On the walk back to my apartment, I stopped by the corner of Momom's block and saw her lights on. I would do anything to be in that warm house right now, eating take out while she cleaned out my cuts. I just wanted her to hug me and tell me she loved me and that everything was okay.

But here I was, bleeding on a fire hydrant while Justin found rainwater to fill his syringe with. I lost my prized possession, got robbed, then jumped and pistol whipped. I had fucking nothing anymore.

When I got home I called Viktoriya and cried my eyes out. Why did I do this? How could I let this happen? October had always been a horrible month and I should've known something bad would happen; I should've been prepared for the worst and shouldn't have been so stupid.

I didn't mean to be a junkie and sell my necklace. I just had to get high because I couldn't fucking stop. I loved the thrill of getting money, the nervousness of going to your dealer..I loved the feeling of something going in my nose. I didn't mean to hurt my mother and break her heart. I just needed to feel better, I couldn't be sick anymore. I couldn't take it for even a fucking hour.

And then the strangest thing happened. I emptied out the massive pile of dope and snorted it, and then nodded out on the phone with Viktoriya five minutes later. One Camden bag stamped 7UP made me nod out so bad I barely had time to clean the blood off my face before my mother came home.

I lit a cigarette, thinking to myself that it was all worth it before I fell asleep in bliss. I messaged Jordan to let him know what happened, to let him know I tried my best to get money for when I see him next.

"Omg Kayla, are u okay???? Why would you do that? Are you hurt bad? I'll see u tomorrow ok I love u but btw don't post about us hanging out on fb or anything cause my mom or sister will see it."
That was the last thing he wrote to me, and I never saw him again.

For months I cried over him, making sure to message him multiple times a day, always making sure to defend his name...and this is what happened. I would never see him again. My habit only got worse, and I could no longer deny it to my mother or friends. Everyone knew and I didn't give a fuck.

I got money anyway I could now. I was working at a little Cafe type of place and was on the register which was perfect at that time. Anytime I rang someone up and they gave me exact change, I would cancel out the order before anyone could see and stash the cash in my bra. One time a guest left his wallet and iPhone - those were both mine and drained of funds within literal seconds.

I was going to D by myself now, fuck Brian and Brenda. D drove to me, and worst case I'd walk to him - fuck being scared of the neighborhood. Nothing scared me anymore after that night on Jersey St. I didn't care about shit anymore. My usual dealers were also now David and Marie because that's just how fucking pathetic my life was. They were back together, and for some crazy reason living at John's father's house. John's father bought Marie a car, and together she and David would do their heroin deliveries in it. I'd be so sick I didn't give a fuck. I'm sure Marie got off on it. Taking my man AND my money - what else was her's for the picking?

They had a soft spot for me, of course. They'd trade me packs of cigarettes for bags (the 3 packs of cigarettes Momom dropped off to me always lasted more than the money) and had no minimum usually. The only time they'd threaten me and run their mouth is when I wouldn't go to them because they took too long. I couldn't wait when I was sick, I refused.

It was late November, early December and I was an addict now, there was no dying that anyway it came at me. While I was barely able to make it to the bathroom half the time, I'd hold back bile to snort my bags - laid out 4 at a time now. Gone long were the days that I could only handle one at a time, and replacing them were days that I loved to do 4 in each nostril - I loved the drip, and I loved the feeling of my nose being clogged with dope.

Scott kind of started to hang out with me again, but not as a friend anymore. Instead, he'd pick me up, take me across the bridge for cigarettes and buy my Red Velvet Lattes, forcing me to put my money away. It was really, REALLY fucking nice...until he'd put his fat hand on my thigh, asking when we'd go on a date. I just wanted my friend back and apparently, the only way to have that was to let him hit on me. So I'd laugh and gently remove his hand, telling him we were always better off as friends. I'd try to bring up the old days to prove my point.

"Remember how I was your 'co-pilot'? Or how you always picked me up after my shifts at the diner, and your parents knew to make a plate for me because I never had food at home? Or what about this, remember that?" It never worked. His brain could only handle one thing at a time and I should've known that; I should've known he only wanted one thing from me. At this point in my life, that's all guys ever fucking wanted.

Anytime I tried mending my broken heart and pushing my fear away and let a boy in, something fucked up happen. They'd shove their hands down my pants, calling me pet names and telling me how different and unique I was; they always left when I told them I didn't want to do anything.

Since Viktoriya moved back, life was kind of better. She always made sure to get enough money for me if she was gonna get high, or if she went and did shit with Ray she made sure to do enough so I wouldn't be sick.

And then, one time she hit me up knowing I was sick. She told me Ray had shit and was willing, and asked if I wanted to come along. My fingers froze in their place, unable to pick out a correct answer. Selling myself was against my moral; it was against my religion of living. I couldn't do it. I couldn't live with myself.

But I was also very, very sick. Momom was outta cash and my mother was having none of my shit. 'It's close to Thanksgiving' she yelled, 'I need money for fucking food.' Even though she and I both know she wouldn't cook. I sighed, pressing my fingers to my temple. I needed money. I didn't wanna throw up anymore - I couldn't. I couldn't live like this anymore.

"What do I have to do? I don't really wanna touch him." I replied back, fearing the response I was gonna get. Was I really going to do this? Because I fucking refuse, but anything is better than being sick.

"Nothing. I'll make sure you don't have touch him. Maybe a back rub, but I promise that's it, baby." And that was that. I was so fucking relieved I wouldn't have to do anything against my morals that I immediately said okay. Viktoriya wouldn't push me past my limits, she'd just make sure I was high and that if Ray got a little *too* hot and bothered with her I'd stop him. I was okay with that.

So Ray picked me up in his stupid red 90's sports car a few minutes later, and that was it. We made stupid jokes and walked in his house, one of the many beautiful row homes that surrounded Lambert Street, adjacent to 29. It was a horrible fucking neighborhood, but I'd kill to have that view of the Delaware. The lights bounced off the perfect way, and the fact it was winter time made it that type of quiet that made even the worst of neighborhoods beautiful. I loved it. I loved everything about it.

His mother sat on the couch in his home, watching 2 kids that weren't his but raised as if they were. I knew of the mother of the children and made small chat, remarking to Ray's old mother how cute and shy they were.

We descended into his room that was also the basement, and every step I took was careful. I didn't want him to confuse anything I did with being interested. I was fucking terrified, and I hope he knew it. I barely spoke, something rare, and only laughed when I had to.

"Give me the shit first." Viktoriya made sure he knew why we were there, and he was okay with that. At first, he only gave us 6 bags, then through the night we were handed more. I did all 3 of mine right off the bat.

We made small talk and at first, it wasn't bad. Ray wasn't *completely* creepy, anyway. He was a normal guy with normal, heart break type problems. The two kids upstairs were, without a doubt, definitely not his. He didn't know about the oldest not being his until he came out half-black, and the other one he believed was his until a crack head randomly called him up and said he hooked up with the baby momma in rehab. He loved her, and you could tell, but he wasn't clean, and she was just getting her shit together. He'd take care of the kids every fucking day if he had to.

And then it slowly happened after he smoked a gram of crack. I don't know if it was because the dirty man in him came out, or if he was just tweaking really hard and needed to concentrate, but it came creeping. It started with him laying on the bed, belly down, asking Viktoriya and me for a back rub. I looked at her, then back to his greasy body, then back to her and panicked. But all she did was say no, and quietly in Russian told me it's okay not to touch him.

Then he turned over, now his back was on the bed and Viktoriya was straddled on top of him, rubbing his shoulders and running her hands over his collarbones. I gagged, blamed it on the dope, and demanded more. I couldn't do this. I shouldn't of fucking came here tonight. I should've said no, I should've -

"Kiss," Ray moaned out, making the hair on my body stand straight. "Kiss each other in front of me."

"Oh my god, Viktoriya." I breathed out. I wasn't ready for this. I knew when it came down to it, I wouldn't be able to touch him..but she was my best friend...and I liked men. I didn't wanna be the type of girl who goes to parties and makes out with chicks because it was fun, and I certainly didn't wanna be the one who did it for heroin. I couldn't do this.

I looked to his dirty, crack and heroin infested coffee table. There was another bundle on it just waiting for me and her to split. I'd be sick tomorrow without it since I already did my wakeups. I needed it. She wouldn't let me steal it, either; his crack induced paranoia would know right away.

"Just quick, one, two, three, peck." She whispered, going back to rubbing Ray and telling him how sexy I was. I loved her. She was the only person in the world who protected me anymore, and I know she would never force me to do anything I didn't want to...but right now, I felt fucking stuck.

I looked at her, then to Ray. His eyes were rolling in the back of his head because his high and Viktoriya's fingers felt that good. I shuddered, biting the lip ring that was pierced in my top lip. It was now or never, and I wanted to leave as soon as I fucking could. If I did this, that would happen. Viktoriya would force him to take us home, and that would be it.

So I did it. I leaned over and kissed her, making Ray's body shake and say something completely unintelligible.

Maybe it wasn't a big deal, and maybe to other people that was fucking nothing. But to me, and still to me, it was everything. I sold out, I sold my fucking morals for a bundle of heroin even if it was a kiss that lasted 20 seconds with my best friend. I did it because a man told us to, and because a bundle of heroin was on the line.

A lot of people told me not to include that part. A lot of people told me I would look bad, and people would look down on me, but I don't care. That's what heroin does to you, and my point is to fucking scare people. What I did was fucking scary, no if's and's or but's. Sometimes when I'm at work, I think about it. Whenever I see Viktoriya on the 'people you may know' on Facebook, I think about it. It haunts me every day, and I *want* people to know that. I want people to know how badly it fucked me up.

Ray took us home after that, and Viktoriya and I said nothing about it ever again. The next day before she left, she gave me 40 dollars.

"You know that guy that keeps hitting you up on the book, Tank?"

I nodded my head. Tank was a lonely, 30-something white guy who lived in Levittown with his parents. His comments still linger on my Facebook photos, some 3 years later.

"You will never, ever have to do anything with him, I promise you that. But if you ever need money, you sweet talk him and he'll be at your door in 15 minutes."

After the night before, that sounded like heaven. She told the truth, too. Whenever I was out of money options I'd hit up Tank. A quick message calling him 'sweetie' and how I needed 60 dollars for my rent or my landlord would kick me out always worked. Sometimes I'd hit him up 3 days out of the week, the same excuse always flowing out of my mouth. I never had to hug him. I never had to kiss him. I never even had to get in his fucking car. He'd just put the money in my palm, sincerely tell me how sorry he is this was happening, and leave. If he offered anything under 30$ I'd whine, saying that wasn't good enough and I couldn't talk to him because I had to pack - that worked the best. He hustled for money, then sped over the bridge to my apartment. It never not worked.

I got braver with asking random's for money. Any guy that was non-stop messaging me got the generic 'I can't talk, I need to find 40$ or I'll lose my apartment.' I worked my story nonstop, always sounding more and more pathetic with the next guy. I was fucking unstoppable.

I hated men at this point. I didn't try to let anyone in because I just couldn't give a fuck. I wanted money, and I didn't want to touch you for it - there lies the problem. My heart still ached and I was convinced only heroin could fix it.

Heroin never left me. Heroin always found a way to visit me, to tell me he loved me. He was handsome and always called for me, I just couldn't answer sometimes. Even if heroin only loved me for my money, I still loved him. He was the only person I let into my heart; he was the only person I would never let go. He made me feel better, he made the world beautiful. He calmed my PTSD and made me feel like a functioning member of society. I loved him so fucking much.

If I wasn't with Viktoriya, I was with John. He'd save his tips from working delivery at Domino's and come to visit me every few days, driving us to Stuyvesant to cop. He was cheap on his bags, though, only giving me two or three when he bought bundles on bundles or even bricks. After a while, I would rob him and blame it on the dealer.

One time, I set it up with David and Marie. They'd bring me the real dope and help me package the fake shit to give to John. Even if David and John grew up together, they were always feuding; David got off on shit like this and I used it to my advantage. I didn't care how close John and I were, he was a fuck boy for trying to give me as few bags as possible and he needed to learn his lesson every single fucking time we copped. I stole bundle upon bundle from him, apologizing for the dealer each time. He never caught on like the fucking idiot he was.

When John and Viktoriya were out, I was with Cristine. She had a guy just like Tank, except he drove us to cop and was much closer to our area. We would get high, remark how cute the bands around the bags or how cool the stamp was, then nod out on my couch until it was time for her shift at the strip club across the bridge.

My days were always the same. Wake up (sometimes) sick, hustle for money, cop, nod out until my mother gets home, hide the evidence two minutes before she comes in, repeat. I was getting tired of it, tired of the repetition, tired of not doing anything with my life. The cafe fired me, my dealers were my ex boyfriend and the woman that stole him away, and my 4 best friends were heroin addicts that shot up and nodded out in my house. My upstairs neighbor's scummy husband stole my laptop, my flat screen TV, my rent money; we couldn't do anything because my mother had a warrant and insisted they'd pick her up or they'd jump us. I tried to insist that they wouldn't, that we were friends because of how close we got but honestly, I was starting to believe her myself. We had no food, no cable, and weren't allowed to put the heat on past 63 degrees. I was miserable every goddamn day of my life.

I wasn't hiding my addiction very well. Momom was getting bothered that I kept asking her for money, I had robbed all of my options, and was getting nastier than usual. I tried fighting everyone and anyone and sold whatever I could. Fake weed? I had it. Fake mushrooms, Molly, Roxy's? I was the supplier.

I didn't wonder how I got this way anymore, or how I turned into this new form of Kayla. I just accepted it and figured that everyone else had to, too. If they didn't they wouldn't have to be in my life, as simple as that. I stopped giving a fuck, and if you still did you were the silliest person on Earth.

Chapter Twelve

December 2013, Thinking I was cute as fuck with grey skin.

Christmas hit like a ton of bricks. Before I knew it, Cristine had her chauffeur guy take us all over Trenton so I could cop before my mother's grandmother's Christmas Eve party. It had been a tradition that I'd been going to since I was born, and tonight was not the night I would skip it. Heroin addict or not, I had shit to do. I was still functioning, after all.

I got dressed the best as I could, which included a cardigan that was just long enough to cover my new hand tattoo from my mom's dad (Popop Puppy, confusing yet?), and a pair of fucking yoga pants with my uggs. But I thought I looked good; I thought I looked functioning and classy. In reality, I was as classy as a heroin addict who lived in Trenton, New Jersey could get.

We got there in no time, making small talk with my Popop Puppy on the way. We walked up the large driveway with presents (that my Popop had bought) in hand, kissing cousins who we haven't seen since last year and saying hello to everyone we possibly could.

At first, it was fun, truly, honestly, 100 percent pure fun. I snuck off to the bathroom to do my dope and came back down still just as happy. The only cousin I'm close to is 10 year old Isabella, but catching up with everyone while I was still coherent was amazing. Some had kids, some just bought houses, some were just drunk.

But somewhere within talking to family is where the depression creeps out and grabs your neck. It reminds you that you're not even close to this side of the family. It reminds you that they are more successful than you; they are more happy, far better off than you. They have siblings to love, even space heaters in their rooms to warm them up when their California King's get cold. They can eat whenever they want and always keep in contact with each other.

My family was always the odd ones. I was rejected by the group of kids when I was young and didn't have a mommy to help open my presents when the adults told us it was time. I was the weak one, the one who got made fun of for having a lisp and being chubby. Natural Selection worked in the way it usually works with kids, and I was the unknowing prey.

Just like that, I had to leave. I ran up to the bathroom and did the last of my bundle, getting to that point of my high where I was confidence again and *had* to make sure Facebook knew how good I looked. I was getting risky, more confident in my decisions and that was always when my addiction got dangerous. I looked at the envelope my Popop Puppy gave me for Christmas - 200$. That was my present. 200 dollars that was supposed to go on a shopping spree but would go to a brick of heroin either by tonight or early tomorrow.

Now getting agitated by my lack of dope, I rushed down the stairs, telling my mother I wanted to leave because I felt uncomfortable and she agreed. She somehow conned my Popop Puppy into taking us home, and on the way to my apartment stopping at the 711 to pick up Newports and call my dealer. They were more than happy to come through; they were getting high on their own supply, and their profits were dwindling down to none.

Just like that, my Christmas Eve was over. Christmas was gone from my memories almost completely, the only thing I remember are flashes of going to Aunt Jen's for presents and then Momom's, then leaving happily with the clothes and money I got.

I don't remember the days that passed, just that I was so fucked up and ran out of heroin on the 28th. I ran out of a brick of heroin in 4 days. 5 bundles gone in 4 days. I guess in retrospect that wasn't so bad, my habit was now at a bundle a day...but just thinking about how quick it went still shocks me.

On the 28th of December, an old friend I knew from the days I hung out with the kid with the cool basement hit me up and asked if I wanted to go there. I said okay, thinking we were all gonna hang out and I was more than happy to have the company.

They picked me up outside the apartment as I kissed my mother goodbye, telling her I would see her when she got back from Mike's on the weekend (he didn't live with us.)

"Yo..d-d...d-did you bring the diesel?" Haven asked, slurring his words due to the cheap Majorska he had downed before coming to get me with everyone else.

"The fuck?" I raised my eyebrow. First of all, everyone in this fucking car thought I was clean. Secondly, I don't share my dope with anyone. "No dude, fuck outta here."

He had an attitude after that, calling me a slur of names but I ignored it because I didn't think he would be the main one I was hanging out with.

I was wrong though. As soon as we got to Greg's (kid with the basement), they all started to get ready to go to the bar.

"I can't go to the bar, I'm only 18..." I said quietly, instantly embarrassed as they all laughed at me.

"You're not fucking going to the bar," Haven spit at me. "We were GONNA hang out here...but you haddjaa fuck it up."

I rolled my eyes at his drunk ass as I devised a plot to get back to my apartment. He instantly reminded me how much I hated men, how much I hated hanging out with people, and I needed to leave without punching someone in their dumb ass face.

And then my phone rang that stupid fucking phone rang, and when I checked the caller ID my heart dropped just as it did that year and some months ago. My mother.

"Hello?"

"You wanna tell me why the fuck there's dope bags hidden in your *Harry Potter* book? Huh? Don't you DARE lie to me, Kayla. It's not Jordan's, it's not Brian's, who the fuck is it? Tell me the God damned truth, Kayla Nicole!"

I looked at the scene around me. This basement is where it all kind of started, the whole opiate thing anyway. I had no lies left in me, I could no longer run because my feet were so fucking tired and my body ached every day to be normal again. I told her to hold on and ran out of the house, sitting on Greg's front step before answering.

"It's mine, Mommy. I'm not lying to you. It's all mine." I had finally told her the truth, and once again I was crying. I could no longer hide what was going on, my mouth was getting tired of the fabricated stories it told my own mother.

She herself was sobbing, but in between breathes she managed to spit out for me to get the fuck home and I did just that. Haven started talking shit and I told him I'd knock him the fuck out if he didn't shut up, and told Greg to take me home now. He *denied*, like the piece of shit he is, saying it wasn't his fault I was still doing dope and he had no room.

"Greg, I do not give a FUCK." I spat, looking for his girl friends keys so I could drive myself home. "You're taking me home, and I swear to God it's going to be now."

And they did. They took me home while I was crying in the backseat, begging whatever God I believed in to make this easy. I didn't want rehab. I didn't want to go to a shitty place where I'd hate everyone and have to sleep in a foreign bed. My whole family would know at that point, and if I could leave this to just my mother my plan was set.

As I was getting out of the car, Greg began to say something about rehab and I completely ignored him by shutting the door in his face. I had no time for his shit now.

I walked into the apartment, my shaky legs dragging me to the small bathroom where my mother was curling her short hair for volume. "I-I...I'm home, Mommy."

She turned her head to look at me like the fucking exorcist. At first, she completely ignored me, moving to the living room to sit down on the couch. She wasn't nice at first, not that I don't blame her, but it definitely made things harder. She spat questions out at me, and I answered them as false and quickly as I could. I even showed her the 7 suboxone I had copped a few weeks earlier to prove my point that I really was gonna try to get clean.

"How long have you been using?"

"Six months, since Jordan left."

"Are you shooting? Were those needles yours?"

This time, I was able to tell the truth. "No, mommy. I'm just sniffing."

Her young, beautiful face became more gentle at this point. She sighed and brought me into a hug, kissing me on the crown of my head. "The clinic won't let you in, but I promise as your mother Kayla I will help you with this as much as I can. I will not let you be in pain, and I will not let you suffer."

She kept up on her word. She gave me her 75$ Rainbow gift card that I told her I'd trade for subs (but really dope), and that on Monday she'd find more subs or even Methadone. I was excited -

and not for the methadone, but to actually be clean. I would be well and happy and be able to live my life again.

Brian and Brenda slept over that night, then in the morning took me to the pawnshop downtown to trade my gift card. We got some dope then went back to my apartment.

Sarla, of all people, came over. She was now pregnant and glowing and a change of pace to be around. She was always positive, the only time a smile not on her face was when she was fighting with Dom. I loved her as much as I loved Viktoriya, and together the 3 of us were best friends. I had a group again.

We went to a meeting together and besides my mother, she was the most supportive person I had. She stayed the whole time with me at that meeting, encouraging me to read and to put my hand up when anyone asked if it was anyone's first day clean. I got my first NA chip (besides when I was little and went to meeting with my mother) that day. It never left my hand or my purse, always finding a way for me to show it off. I was happy to be doing this.

A few days passed and it was New Year's Eve. 2013 broke my heart and beat me to the fucking ground, and I was excited to do the same thing to it. I had one plan that night, and it was to get high one last time. Momom gave me a 100$, Viktoriya and Sarla were coming, and I even opened my heart and allowed David and Marie to come over, seeing as they had just lost custody of now 2 kids once again. Marie's face supported a new black eye, and I tried to open my heart out more.

Despite them being there, it was a good night. They left when the ball dropped, and Viktoriya slept over while Sarla stayed until her eyes could no longer stay open. I got high, kissing each bag before emptying them. This was it for me, and I had to make sure I had the last hoorah.

"I'm proud of you, baby," Viktoriya said, moving over so I could share the bed with her. "You're doing the unthinkable for people like us. I'm so happy for you."

And I was, too. We took a New Year's Eve kiss picture for Facebook and went to sleep, the thoughts of what my life can now be filling my dreams.

I was no longer junkie Kayla. I was now clean and serene Kayla; the better, more mature version.

Chapter Thirteen

Sarla kept tabs on me all the fucking time. I don't know if it was because my mother paid her (kidding..kind of), or because we were genuinely friends, but her company helped me through a lot.

The whole suboxone thing fucking sucked, that much was obvious. I wallowed in my own self pity while I waited 16 hours in withdrawal, and when I couldn't take enough I took a half. Then another. And then another. My mother, who's knowledge in opiate blocking drugs reached only to methadone, was clueless and hated it. She had no idea how to get me not sick and it pained her almost as much as it pained me to go through it.

She'd leave for work at 2, leaving me to my own devices with more trust than I deserved. I didn't get high though, not at first. Instead, I put on the white robe Viktoriya gave me, grabbed my pack of Newports, and headed for the couch to sit it out. It was the only time I didn't mind not being allowed to use the heat..and then I saw Foxxy Cleopatra huddling in two blankets and turned it up from its place at 47 degrees Fahrenheit. Around 12:05 at night she'd come home, a look of worry already on her face before she could ask me how today was.

When I had methadone, it was a lot better. It helped me more than the subs ever could, but with that came me wanting to get high again. Methadone, unlike subs, will not put you through immediate withdrawal if you decide to do dope; since I was only doing about 60 mg which is considered under a blocking dose, I'd get fucking blasted. My mom would leave the methadone out for me and go to work, and if I didn't sell it for dope I'd do it and then try to get money.

By January 7th, I was getting high and getting dope sick again. I went through all of that for fucking nothing. You can never get clean if you aren't ready, and I wasn't. I felt like I was being forced and I resented that, and because I resented that I had to 360 everything. I had to take *my* life in *my* hands, not my mother's.

Cristine went missing one day, I hardly listened to the begging's of Brian and Brenda, John moved to Kentucky of all places, and David and Marie were God knows where. They were completely off the map, no longer able to support selling dope because they did all of it up. They sold their car, lost the room they were staying in, and had no kids to take care of again; they just stopped giving a fuck. Just like that, my little group of junkie friends was gone.

I started to date someone new and I really, kinda liked him a lot. His name was Kyle and for some reason his stupid septum piercing and bad tattoos and bad fashion made me so fucking interested. In reality, he was a hipster white kid from a rich part of New Jersey that I had nothing in common with but music, but the fact he was a *struggling heroin addict* made me want to know him more.

We dated from the early days of January until the end of February. Every day I would call John on the phone and cry; I didn't want this man to relapse, but I wasn't ready to get clean, what should I do? I would never want my worst enemy to start heroin, and I know we would break up the second he found out I was getting high again.

So, I did what any sensible person did. I hid it. Viktoriya helped me hide my drug use and for a little while it worked, until he called me out on my bullshit and gave me money to order a bundle. He gave me 8 bags and only did 2. I liked him more.

Brian came out of the blue one day, picking me up from my apartment than going to get Kyle. He had just got his income tax and wanted to stay for a few days at my apartment, but get dope on the way. Sure, whatever, that's just what we did. A red stamp called 'El Cartel' was back around, infamous for being the summer of 2013's best shit; everyone, including Kyle, was excited. Apparently, he remembered it to, and because of that, he bought 80$ worth, giving Brian and I the most while he kept 4 to himself. We went to the room Briand and Brenda were renting and they started their routine of mixing their dope and finding a vein, while my empty-out-4-bags-and-sniff routine was much, much simpler.

Besides the time my dad was almost dead and when I fell out, I had only been around it once and that was with John. Being around someone who's overdosing is one of the scariest things in the world. Any normal human being would try their fucking best to help them - calling 911, CPR, etc. But as a drug addict, we are not normal; our brains are not wired the correct way. We worry about *us,* we worry about what's going to happen to *us.* If we even call 911, we have to hide our shit first, then sometimes if we're low enough search the person who's ODing's pockets for any type of treasure we can discover. I didn't do that when John overdosed, but probably only because I had already robbed him for a bundle on the way back to my apartment.

It happens so fucking quick. I did my bags, Brian shot up, and just as we turned our heads to look at Kyle, his pale acne ridden face turned blue. He fell to the ground, now shaking as bile started to foam out of his mouth. The fucking sounds that came out of his mouth terrify me to this day.

I didn't know what to do, and the look on Brian's face clearly said he didn't either.

We tried picking him up, we tried smacking him, we fucking tried everything. I tried everything I fucking could that day. Glass of water upon glass of water went on top of Kyle's greasy hair and it did nothing, punch upon best right hook I had collided with his face that day and nothing fucking helped.

"We gotta get him to the ER," I yelled shakily, starting to put my dope in my purse.

"And do what?! They'll arrest us on fucking sight." Brian yelled back, pacing back and forth in his tiny room.

"Then we'll fucking leave him." And that was our plan, all thanks to the person who was supposed to be his girlfriend. Brian started to carry him out of the room, leaving me with instructions to grab his phone and all the dope. I found the dope no problem, even snagging a few of Brian's for myself, but his phone was a no show.

I dialed his number, and he answered the phone. Fucking idiot. "Yeah, get the fuck out here he's waking up."

I ran as fast at my legs would let me, meeting Brian at the stairs where he was still dragging Kyle by the legs. "I thought he woke up?!"

"So..did...I" he grunted, motioning for me to grab his head and help carry him.

We somehow maneuvered him to Brian's truck, telling his nosey neighbors that Kyle was just having a seizure because he didn't take his meds. They obviously didn't believe it, shouting things about how we need to watch our tolerance and shit. This freaked Brian out more, in return giving him super junkie strength so he'd be able to put Kyle's almost lifeless body in the backseat.

I hopped in the front seat, strapping on my seat belt and praying to whoever would listen. I lost my best friend Ryan, I lost my mother until I was 9 years old, I saw my dad half dead at such a young age that my brain is seared with images of that day. I couldn't take it anymore. Not today. I looked at Brian. His shaggy hair was all over the place, his shaky, pale fingers desperately trying to buckle his seat belt. He was just as scared.

I turned my body to face Kyle's body in the backseat. His skin got some color back, but not enough to make him look alive. "Please, please, please, don't do this." There was no point in begging, but I was never one to stop talking. "We had a whole fucking weekend planned and you cannot bail out on me, not tonight."

I don't have the voice of an angel. In fact, more times than I'd like, I've been called annoying. But I guess that day I did because somehow, after 20 minutes of bile forming at his purple lips, he woke up. "W..why i-is everyone b-bugging out?"

"Oh my fucking god." And just like that, by the grace of God, he woke up and was fine. He didn't even miss any of the dope I had taken from him.

He left my apartment a few days after, the honeymoon of our month long relationship fizzling out. I was never dope sick for more than 12 hours, but because Kyle threw out my scrapes and refused for me to ask my Momom for money, I was sick for a whole 24 hours. I had to start copping in secrecy, and I no longer wanted anything to do with him. I was back to hating men.

We stopped talking less and less, I was back to getting high by myself and wondering what the fuck I had did wrong for Kyle to not text me as much. Was I really that bad to be around, that fucking annoying? Or was my addiction just slowly pushing people away, their only means of hiding their disgust was by leaving my life? My mind was a living paradox. I hated the kid so much, but couldn't stand the thought of him not talking to me.

I had no answers anymore. When I couldn't get money I would have mental breakdowns and could no longer hide my addiction from everyone. My mother knew, Momom was sick of giving me money. One day I found the Walmart credit card Momom Taco Bell gave me for emergencies; I maxed it out within two weeks, and she cut me off for months. This time, besides Sarla, I truly had nobody.

They say you can feel when something fucked up is about to happen, and I think that's true. I woke up one day and the air was different, thicker, harder to breathe. I found myself having panic attacks for no reason, crying every fucking chance I could get.

And like the devil himself, he came to me. He knocked on my door unannounced, with Robitussin coating his lips and abscesses in the shallows of his skinny, pale arms. Barely coherent, I had no time to say no because he was already letting himself in, crying to my mother about how Marie had left him and how he had nothing. David himself showed up at my door, figuring my apartment would be as good a place of any to live. We said yes.

Chapter Fourteen

Like any other time he unexpectedly came into my life, I felt bad for him. I listened to his horror stories of Marie; of how she robbed him blind, prostituted herself, then came back and made love to him like it was nothing, all just to leave him with a simple note saying 'I have to go. Bye.' I felt bad for him and cleaned up my room, giving him my bed and making sure to give him Immodium and even more cough syrup to try to suppress his withdrawals. My mother found methadone on the streets, and with her own money bought it, dosing him for 3 days so he would get over the worst of it.

I tried to get money for him the first night he was at my apartment, like the fucking idiot I was. I got all my name brand clothes, my North Face jacket, and put them into a garbage bag to pawn off to a place that buys them in the morning. I set up an opportunity to get money, and my mother was even proud of me for trying to get clean once again and taking him in so I would have a constant reminder of what I would be going through.

When he first comes into my life, at first, it's not always bad. He cried every day and I so badly just wanted to scoop him in my arms and take all his pain away - that was my problem. I would never take his dope sick away, but I would try so badly to take the hurt in his heart away; the same hurt he gave me so many years ago when I was baby like.

"I woke up in my cousin Billy's...cause I've been staying there," he began through the hiccups he got from all the cough medicine "and I went to wake Marie up...cause we had to have a plan for the day. We were getting by, by stealing batteries from Home Depot and selling them back. 6 dollars a pack. Kayla, she just wasn't there...she just...left." He was either full sob or full raging maniac by the time he got to the end of the story. Nothing ever helped him besides heroin.

The beginning is not always terrible.

But just like depression, he sneaks up in the shadows and reappears as he's gripping your neck. He will not let you get away, he will not let you ignore him. He is just like depression, anger, and anxiety all in one. He is hell in a 5'4 man.

It started by him complaining he was withdrawing on the 4th day of being dosed on methadone via my mother's money. That's what set me off first, because there was no way in hell he would've felt anything. He just wanted more, so much so that he made us all broke and didn't think twice. He didn't blink when he took all of my mom's bus money for crack, and he certainly didn't think when broke all of my possessions and threw the huge dresser I first ever did heroin on when I refused to steal money of that Walmart credit card. That stand-off ended in him threatening my cat's life, and me sobbing at the cashier's counter as I took 40 dollars out as cash back.

I couldn't just kick him out, it wasn't that simple. He held the threat of telling my mother about my heroin abuse over my head; he held the fact that she apparently liked him better, and as she believed him and was kicking me out, she'd be crying on his shoulders. He was a fucking manipulator, and I was powerless. I was like a battered women. I didn't feel safe in my own home. He was slowly turning my mother against me, he was taking all of my money, destroying all my things. He made me less than him, just so he could survive. I couldn't stand it.

Often, he'd compare me to Marie. Though my affection for him was long gone, every single thing he made fun of me for stung. When I stuck up for myself, it only got worse.

"Marie made herself look so fucking good when she'd hang out with all of the group, how the fuck did you expect me not to jump? While you were busy dressing like a slob with your fat fucking stomach hanging out, she dressed to the fucking nines and made sure I was watching her."

I wouldn't say anything, instead just mumble a whatever and look on the ground for scrapes, or scribble in my journal about how Kyle had broken up with me.

I had Sarla. Sarla was going to pop any day now and Dom was MIA most of the time. She had signed them up for a 7 hour birthing class and I went with her instead, having more fun than he ever would as we tried different birthing techniques and watched how big you dilate. During breaks she'd cry in my arms about how badly it hurt to see everyone with their significant others, so to make her feel better we made a joke that I was the baby's father. It may seem silly, but it cheered her up most of the time. I went to her ultrasound appointments and cried when I saw her daughter move around in her stomach. We would beam when the nurse would tell us how much we reminded her of her and her best friend. We were inseparable, and she tried her best to keep me clean even though I would do bags behind her back and nod out in her car. I'd blame it on sleep deprivation because of David living in my house, and she'd believe me.

David sucked me dry of not only my money, heroin, and cigarettes, but of friends also. Like an unstable boyfriend, he would yell at me to get home or keep me on my cell phone the whole time I was out, or if he thought one was attractive I was to invite them over and be his 'wingman' to help them fuck. That's where I lost my friendship with Viktoriya.

I must have called her a thousand times within the first month David was living with me, crying about how trapped I was and how I didn't know what to do. As the best friend she was, she offered to come sleep over and help me take all the pain away. We would get high, we'd cuddle, we'd sleep and not have anything to worry about if just for one night. In reality, it was the perfect plan, but perfect is not a thing for heroin addicts.

She came over, her beautiful self greeting my mother and then hugging me. We sat in the living room for a while; my mother and I noticed how the tension and dread seemed to be missing and felt as if we could finally breathe. *But perfect does not exist for heroin addicts.*

The door knocked three times, sort of 'tsk, tsk, tsk'; a sort of forewarning, maybe. Of course here came David in all his glory, best outfit and Jordans and everything. I reluctantly let him in my room, Viktoriya grabbing my hand tight all the way there.

"I just got my dead grandpa money." He called the money he got monthly from his family selling his grandfather's estate as 'dead grandpa money.' "I just wanted to pop by. Kayla, why didn't you tell me Viktoriya was here?"

I tried my best to keep it a secret, I truly, honestly, 100 percent did. But I guess one night I must've put my cell phone in a place where he would find it, because he obviously ran through my text's and found out. I didn't want him to ruin this. I wanted just one goddamn night to myself. After everything he put me through, I deserved one night without him.

"It was supposed to be a girls night," Viktoriya answered back quickly, "but that's okay. You can hang out with us for a little bit."

"Actually, Jewel won't let me stay at her house tonight." Jewel was David's sister's best friend who had such a large crush on him that she let him stay at her house night's he didn't stay at mine. "So I'm just gonna stay here. Anyway, Kayla, call up D, order 2 buns."

Just like that, he made himself comfortable, sitting on my bed with his legs spread out. He tossed the money, and Viktoriya trying to leave me some dignity picked it up and gently handed it to me. I called D, who said he's on his way (which in drug dealer time meant 45 minutes) and sat on the futon that was placed across from my bed and just waited.

I was social at first, make jokes and trying my best to be happy. David was on his best behavior, knowing if he turned to his regular piece of shit self I wouldn't 'help him out'. Whatever. I'd rather that than be belittled all night.

But when you get high, that's when things change. Viktoriya shot up, then shot David up because he could never hit a vein. I snorted my bags, lit a cigarette, and hoped I'd get some kind of nod.

And then Viktoriya proposed we cuddle. I took that as me and her, but David thought that he should get involved. I bit my tongue but stayed in my spot against her stomach.

I guess David thought now was the time to lay his moves, because out of his mouth came "Let's give massages", and the way he said it made me know I was not to be involved in this. But what turned my emotions sour was that Viktoriya said okay, and though her hands were touching my back, she let him touch her's.

After a while, I got up from the bed. I was nodding hard, but hearing the two of them talk made me sick and I opted to nodding on my living room couch, mother watching TV or not.

"What are you doing, Kay?" My mom asked, picking her head up from her phone.

"I don't f-fucking know. I'm takin' a nap." So I lit a cigarette and took a nap, adding yet another burn hole to my blanket.

I don't know how long had passed, but I was woken up with dirt covered fingers shaking my body and my mother meekly trying to stop it.

"You're fucking ruining this," David seethed, his lips centimeters from mine. "Get your fat ass up and fucking help me."

"Please, I don't want to," I whined, pulling the covers up to my shoulders. "Please, don't make me do this."

"Get. The. Fuck. In. The. Room."

Like always, I started to cry as I threw the blanket off me. Why did my mother let this happen? Why couldn't she help me in kicking him out? Why did she just watch this go down every fucking day?

Viktoriya was laying on my bed, her dark eyes smiling as they saw me walk in. I sat on the futon, my fingers staying in one place as I tried to figure out how the fuck I would get out of this situation. I had no one to call, no one who would pick me up. I had no relationships with fucking anyone besides Sarla, but I wouldn't let her pick me up. David would never let that happen anyway.

"Let's take a picture for Facebook!" Viktoriya called, pushing her cheek close to mine. I made the signature duck lips, really not knowing what else to make, as I watched David began to shy an arm around her shoulders. I involuntarily shuddered.

I don't know how it happened, or even why. I just remember getting pushed off the bed by *someone,* and because of that I finally had enough. I wasn't allowed to leave the room, but I'd disengage myself all fucking night. I sat down in my closet, big enough for its own bed, and took refuge there. I nodded out there, I smoked cigarettes there.

My phone went off in my hands. '*Are you mad at me, baby?*'

I looked up to see Viktoriya's beautiful face frowning. It's not that I was mad at her, I was mad at the situation I was in. She knew how ex#1 was, and here she was, just completely enabling him. She could've pushed him away, she could've said no, she could've said anything to defend me...but she didn't. She just let it all happen, smiling her big ass smile the whole time. I wasn't mad, but I was fucking hurt. I felt like I had finally lost.

'*No, princess. I'm not.*'

I woke up the next morning with Viktoriya already gone and David waiting only until I woke up to leave.

"You had to fuck everything up, didn't you? Are you fucking jealous, like I don't understand."

I looked at the clock. 8:15 A.M. I was sick, needed to get a wake up, then get dressed for my new job at Shoprite. I put on my glasses, now cracked in the middle because of David, then looked straight into his blue eyes.

"I didn't do shit." It was the truth. To me, anyway. To him I was lying my fucking ass off and he wouldn't have any of that.

"I was just about to get shit in, and you had to ruin it by fucking crying in the closet. Are you fucking dumb?"

I shook my head. "No. I'm not dumb."

"You have to be because I literally cannot fucking contemplate what you did last night." His vocabulary got larger the more mad he got. While fighting and calling you an idiot, he would make you trip over your fucking words so he'd seem like the intelligent one in the argument. He left you no entry ways to win; no words could ever clear yourself from his fucked up brain.

"I need to go to work," I mumbled, grabbing my dope and straw and retreating to the bathroom.

I got to work at around 10, then at 1 I got to go on my 15 minute break. My phone went off the hook. It was Viktoriya.

"We were supposed to be best friends. I didn't want to fuck David last night. I was there for you. But you go and tell him I'm just a dirty prostitute anyway, that I have diseases? You fucking tell him I fuck anyone? That I'll be nothing but a stripper?"

I didn't read the rest, instead just letting my shaky fingers type to deny the whole thing. I had never said a bad thing about Viktoriya all my life. She was the one person in the world I loved the most. I would never try to hurt her. She was the only thing that brought light into my life, besides that day I saw Sarla's daughter on screen. This wasn't fair.

"Save it. Have a good life."

That night was the last time I ever saw Viktoriya. An almost 4 year friendship ruined because of my drug addict ex boyfriend. A few months later I talked to her again, but our relationship wasn't as strong. She cut me off again one day out of the blue. Last time I heard, she was in North Carolina. Meth is her new thing, and I worry about her every day of my life.

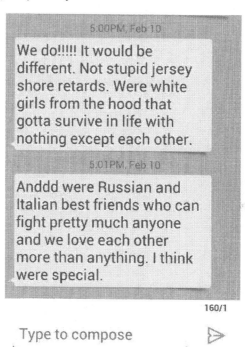

We do!!!!! It would be different. Not stupid jersey shore retards. Were white girls from the hood that gotta survive in life with nothing except each other.

Anddd were Russian and Italian best friends who can fight pretty much anyone and we love each other more than anything. I think were special.

160/1

Type to compose

From just a little over two months before that night.

Chapter Fifteen

On a good day, I was able to lie to David and tell him I had to stay at work longer than I really had to. Momom would take me home, give me money, then I'd call D and get high all to myself. I treasured those days the most, the ones where I didn't have to share my dope or my cigarettes.

On a bad day, which was more frequent, I had to share everything.

David would make me shoot him up, cursing at me the whole time because I would take too long. For some reason, he could never do it himself and depended on a fucking sniffer to do his shooting. I didn't understand that.

Then, he'd smoke all the cigarettes, making me feel like shit when I'd ask him to cut down because it was the end of the month and Momom didn't have any more money. He would remind me how I helped him spend all his money (I was always to scared to, but regardless), and proceed in his actions.

Then right around the time before we went to sleep (it was now April, and more nights than none he stayed with me) he'd make us walk all around Trenton for cigarette butts. The first stop was a bar a few blocks down from my apartment called Tir Ra Nog. After that, it was the local Quick Chek, that usually proved to have more. He would be a few feet ahead of me, pretending not to be with me as I had to search along the concrete for 'good' butts, or ask random strangers for some. If I was hysterically crying by how much of a piece of shit he made me feel, strangers would feel worse and give me 2 - one for me, and one to shut him up and hopefully be easy to the sick and crying girl in front of them. People took pity on me. I hated it.

I got money from Tank one more time before he kind of caught on, then blocked him. I had to rob two friends I've had since I was 14. I found a wallet at Shoprite, stole it, had the cops called, and had to plant it back without being found. I hid in my bathroom to smoke or do the dope I somehow hid from David.

I had, at this point, been using dope for 2 years and my habit was now at two bundles, or 20 bags, a day.

I thought back to the beginning a lot. How I'd get high with Jordan, cruise down 95 with Scott and everyone, and not have a single care in the world. Money never ran out, and I usually was always surrounded by love.

But here I am now, 2 years later. Living in almost a fucking drug den while my first ever boyfriend manipulates and scares my mother and I into letting him live with us. I was no longer doing dope to get high, at this point I was just doing it to get well. I didn't have a cell phone, because David made me sell it for dope. I had nothing.

John came up from Kentucky to visit, apparently stealing a car and telling his mother to go fuck herself. He didn't want to live in the south because there wasn't *good* heroin, which sucked for someone like him because he was only doing it to get high, not well like his oldest best friends. He was happy to see us, even after we robbed him the week prior via him wiring us money for dope we would never send him. He never fucking learned.

The first day was fun, for John, anyway. He would beg us to go 'bombing' (aka using shitty markers and graffiting everywhere), then get cigarettes and dope and have to split it down the middle with all 3 of us.

He had fun until about his fifth day in New Jersey. At that point, David wouldn't let him hang out with anyone, and unless he had money he got treated like shit. Just because he wasn't me, doesn't mean he was exempt for getting treated like pond scum. Because he was John, and because he had known David for so long, he was actually more of a target. David would make fun of him, then look at me to join in.

And I would. I'd make fun of John and make him feel like a piece of shit because it got the treatment off of me. It was low, and it was fucking sad, but John didn't even need to be here. He could leave and go to his beautiful suburban home and be treated like royalty and eat as much as he wanted and play video games and watch cable TV. But he wouldn't because, for some sick reason, he wanted to live this lifestyle more than anything. I never understood why.

One night, I had gotten my own dope from D and was nodding out by the grace of God, until David showed up with John. Apparently, they had gotten bad shit because David was everywhere, screaming that their dude gave them dope mixed with suboxone. It didn't make sense to me then, and it still doesn't. There's literally just no possible fucking way, but he insisted; John was a liar for feeling like he did get high, and I wouldn't know because I was a sniffer. In reality, he was just an actor, and would play the role of being sick until he got more heroin in his veins.

He banned John to my room, telling him not to come out until he got a lick for more than 20 bucks. I, on the other hand, was told to make dinner like the female I should be more of. The only food I had was in my freezer, and it was old chicken from November of the previous year. I made it anyway, smiling to myself as the gray parts of the chicken got covered up with Teriyaki sauce.

When the dinner didn't work, he started to pull his pants down, making snapping motions to his dirty boxers. I swallowed my spit, stuttering as I was trying to make up an excuse.

"Don't act like you're not going to do it." He smirked, taking a fistful of my hair and jamming me down to his crotch. He smelled fucking horrendous, and I started to hold back the sobs that danced in the back of my vocal chords.

And right as he was taking his dick out, John came out, saying he found a lick but he didn't want to do it because it was a girl he dated that he was still friends with. David made him anyway, laughing in his face as he pulled up his pants.

"You shoulda never told me, then. But good job, tell her we'll be there in 20." He started taking empty dope bags, folding them together and making it look like it was 2 buns.

We sped down 95, making our way to exit 8 in less than 15. We turned into the apartment complex, John shutting his lights down low as he parked by a field that would lead to our escape.

"Do not talk to her, do not let her see it, do not let her count it. Do you understand?" David asked, putting the fake shit inside cellophane.

John simply nodded, too scared to really do anything else.

"I'm dead ass. If you fuck this up, *you're* getting fucked up, then going to find me money any way you can."

The robee came out of her apartment door, taking long strides to the car. She greeted John happily, making small conversation as John pressed his lips tight, as if scared to say something to fuck this up. He muttered out a 'hi', taking the fake bun out of his jean pocket and fumbling to hand it to her.

It almost reached her hand. Almost. He dropped it right on her fake uggs. Everything seemed to move slow after that.

"You're a fucking idiot!" David shouted, unbuckling his seatbelt and positioning himself across John to try to reach the bags. John stuttered, trying to make a joke as the robee scoffed.

"Don't talk to him like that!"

"Ayo, you know who you talking to?" David asked, his head going up straight. Why did she have to talk back? Didn't she fucking know? Couldn't she fucking tell how vicious he could be by how scared John and I were?

"Obviously no one important." She retaliated, turning her phone light on to look for the fake drugs with John.

"On my set, you can get your jaw rocked," he said with a smirk, pointing an index finger at me.

Before I could even open my mouth, John shouted out that he found it, quickly pushing the girl's fingers away. She didn't bother to reply, either because she didn't know there was a female in the car or because she didn't want to deal with it, I'll never know.

I called D on the way back to Trenton, hoping I'd get at least a few bags even though I had a few from earlier in the day hidden in my closet. Good thing I did, because David shot 9 of them and threw John one. He tried protesting, his strongest argument that he did the robbing but it didn't work. It never would, and he never understood that.

I saw John only one more time. Someone who was my best friend from when I was 14, and someone who I only got closer with via a dope habit, simply left. He didn't tell anyone. He just grabbed his shit, stole his car keys back from his dad, and left.

The last time I saw him he dropped me off a black suitcase. It was the kind of suitcase you see in heist movies; hard and black, and when you opened it up the item of intense desire was in styrofoam casing. Black, to match the suitcase, of course. And just like the heist movies, the item of intent was a black hand gun.

I knew nothing about guns, and it was obvious. I shot a gun a few times, a carbine and something else when I went with Jess to her parents' properties in the mountains of New York. A beautiful, secluded place about 5 hours away, no one gave a fuck what you did. Especially not their family, they had one of the biggest pieces of property around. Besides riding dirtbikes and shooting guns, their favorite pastime was getting drunk in front of a larger-than-life fire pit that overlooked said the actual mountains. You were higher than the fucking clouds. Oh, and one time I even held a gun for David and Justin when I was like 16 and doing the whole side chick thing, but that was really it.

My eyes grew large and I quickly snatched the suitcase. "Why the fuck is he bringing this into my house?"

"I don't know, dude!" John had those corny glasses that changed to sunglasses when it got bright out. Unfortunately for him, they burned out and were always stuck on the sunglass part. "He told me he was going to sell it."

I rolled my eyes, shooing John back to his car as I began to sneak through the back door. My mother was always lax, but this and heroin would be on her crazy fucking shit list, with reason, of course. I moved all the clothes around on the closet floor, making a sort of hole to put the suitcase into. I piled all the clothes back on it, shutting the door and making sure the latch was done before I got ready to go out for the night.

David was out, gone somewhere I didn't really give a fuck about because it gave me a chance to run the town with whoever would give me the chance. So some random picked me up, someone I used to hang out with back when I was sober and trusted enough not to try to touch me. When I got done smoking all of his weed and drowning my sorrows with his Jack Daniels, I hinted that I had to go home. On the ride home my mother called me, and I was too fucked up to care that she probably found more heroin bags.

"Hello?"

"Tell me the truth. I won't be mad." That's how this always fucking went, and she always got mad. "I went in your closet, and I saw this black suit-"

I stopped listening. My heart dropped into my stomach and I had to hold back throw up. She found the fucking gun in my closet. Oh my god. She found the fucking gun. She was going to call the cops, I was gonna go to rehab and then to jail. Oh my god. Oh my god, oh my god.

"What the fuck is wrong with him to bring a fucking gun in our apartment? I didn't even touch it, Kayla. I was too scared too, I won't even lie to you. I put it back in your closet. Tell him to pick it up, and leave it at that."

That was it. Her mental state was slowly deteriorating (thanks to me, no doubt) and she just could not handle what was going on in her house. She could only let it go, because that's all her body could handle. She finally gave up, something a mother could only do when she knew she could no longer help her child. It didn't hurt me so much then, because heroin and Jack Daniels and pot made life beautiful and all my problems disappear, but as I got older I'd apologize for it every day of my life it seemed.

I got back to my apartment and as expected, David and one of his random friends were waiting on my porch. I stumbled to the door, unlocking it as I told them I'd meet them around back.

"He's picking it up now," I told my mother, not waiting in the living room for his response.

I took the suitcase out of my closet, wrapping my sleeve around my hand as I held it so I wouldn't get fingerprints on it. My paranoia was the only thing keeping me from getting arrested a second time.

I placed the suitcase on my mom and I's washer-and-dryer-in-one, then unlocked the back door motioning for the both of them to come in. David walked in first, running his fingers on the front of the suitcase before unlatching the lock and opening. He smirked, looking at his friend.

"She's clean, no bodies, nothin."

The man sucked his teeth, crossing his arms. "It's little, dog. I ain't tryna have somethin' that small."

"Dog, you're not gonna have a better price for something clean like this." He was getting mad, and it wasn't hard to tell. If he didn't sell this gun, he'd have no heroin money, no money to get well. He'd be fucked, I'd be fucked in return, and the process would begin a day early. "120, right now."

"120?!" The man's voice got louder, making my head snap towards him and make a 'shh' noise. He apologized, lowering his voice. "I'll give you 80 right now, shit ain't worth any more than 60 and you know it, bro."

The bickered back and forth, my eyes jumping from one face to another. When I wasn't being a yenta I was checking my phone, pulling up my text messages every two minutes to see whether or not D texted me back with the three simple letters that became my favorite: "omw."

"Damn bro alright, 80." And that was that. David did the exchange, taking the 80 in return for a gun with no bodies. The man started checking out the gun, inspecting all the nooks and cranny's as David counted his money to make sure it was all straight.

"David," I whispered, now annoyed that D didn't text me back. "Do you have any shit on you I can buy or nah?"

He smiled, his overlapped two front teeth showing. "Nah. You don't?"

I shook my head, and he shrugged his shoulders. "Damn, that's beat for you then."

I rolled my eyes, muttering a goodbye as him and his friend exited my apartment. I had a wakeup, and money for tomorrow at least, so tonight wasn't horrible. The gun was gone, making the weight of the world disappear from my mother and I's shoulders. We'd be able to go to sleep a little less scared. A little less scared of dying, a little less scared of being raided, a little less scared of our lives being completely out of control.

A few days later, the guy that bought the gun died due to gun violence on the same street I got jumped and pistol whipped. Authorities say they found a gun on him, too. Every time we got a knock on the door, my mother and I would freeze in our spots. She was already paranoid, making us crawl on the floor whenever the police were at the apartment for the neighbors, but this made it worse. Anybody who was in my apartment the time the cops came was not allowed to talk, or even use their cellphones. All the lights had to be off, and you couldn't breathe loud in fear of them hearing us. I used to joke, saying this is how my ancestors were treated during World War II, but she never thought it was funny. I guess I wouldn't either.

Chapter Sixteen

It was the night before Easter. David, this kid Richard we both knew since before we even dated, and I sat in a circle. They were smoking crack, passing the pipe to and from each other while I was collecting scrapes for the morning to come. I had one wakeup bag, not the regular 4 I needed, and knew I'd be hurting.

"Smoke this," David commanded, filling the pipe with a 10 piece.

"I don't like crack, though." I thought about to when I was younger, to the time right before I did dope and even began with hard drugs. I loved ecstasy, but coke didn't really do it for me. I knew it was different, but I was fucking scared. I was scared to try anything new the first time.

"You became such a fucking baby when you started doing dope," Richard stated simply, now beginning to mix dope inside a bottle cap.

"Just fucking do it." David would not take no for an answer, so as I started to protest the dirty pipe was already in my hands.

"Make sure none of it falls out, and you have to hold it like this," he steadied my hands, then tilted my head at a weird position. "Now breathe in until I tell you, okay? Don't fucking stop, or you're gonna waste a whole fucking 10."

I made sure my hair was behind my back, and as he started to light it I closed my eyes and breathed in as hard as I could until I was told not to. Fuck me for having asthma, right?

After what seemed like five minutes, he told me to stop and I reopened my eyes. I don't remember much, just that my messy room seemed to become a lot gentler, a lot less scary looking.

Pop. Popopopopop. My head kept popping, with every noise it made the more I felt like I was on a cloud that made my emotions overly happily. I was overly-giggly.

"I don't think she wasted it, dude." Richard was always kind when it came to just me. But when he was around David, he was just as much as a piece of shit as him. They were like a fucking team. Instead of telling me I'd be alright and that if I was freaking out I shouldn't, he just *had* to announce I didn't waste it. Whatever.

"Why don't we ever just smoke crack instead of do dope? I wanna do this forever." I exclaimed as if I had made a new junkie discovery.

"We should. You don't get sick, and it's a lot cheaper and lasts longer than dope." It was the first time I had ever been right, or even been agreed with since he barged into my life two months ago.

He was also completely fucking wrong.

With crack, it's not that you get sick, because you don't, but it's about your mental health. Crack will send you to a psych ward off a week-long binge. Crack will make you kill your grandmother for another hit, whereas heroin will only make you rob her. Crack lasts only five minutes, if that, and is a harder dragon to chase. I've seen people have ten years sober from heroin, but it's the fucking crack that makes their knee's weak.

"My arm feels funny," Richard mumbled, moving his arm in kind of a wave.

I laughed until I couldn't anymore, getting a free bag of dope from David for the come down. I had to save it for tomorrow. Easter was more important than a shitty come down. I've been through worse, after all.

I woke up the next day, getting up early enough to do my wakeup and some scrapes. I was going to my Aunt Kathy's, Momom's sister, and they weren't the kindest of people. Aunt Cynthia would be there with her husband and two perfect soccer playing blonde hair and blue eyed daughters. Following in line were my other perfect cousins via Aunt Kathy, Sam, and Nicole. Also blonde haired and blue eyed, they were both going to Rutgers or some prestigious school like that, living in their own places while working towards degrees in *hospitality* or *teaching*.

My family never fit in. Momom was the oldest of all 7 of her siblings, and the first to catch the disease known as addiction. They followed suit, but since they were closer to everyone but her, they bonded together over it. Momom was just an outcasted junkie who never truly got help to them. Even though she hasn't picked up in the bottle in more years than I've been alive, depression medicine still makes her a bad person.

This was the first real year my mother was allowed at the house. They didn't trust her *junkie mentality*, but her lost cause daughter could stay. She'd just have to eat at the children's table and not talk much while everyone else fawned over Sam and Nicole or Aunt Cynthia's kids.

That's just how it's always been.

I was to sit and stay in my place while Aunt Cynthia made sly, snarky comments my way and Momom tried desperately to establish a real connection between her sisters. *Where was I going to school? Do I have a boyfriend? Where do I work? Did I get my GED yet, even? How could you *even* get your ears that stretched? I would never!* I would never want to be around you, but here I am now. Remember that year you told me I couldn't go in your kitchen because your snowflake daughters were scared of my outfit? Bitch.

Now taking place at the kid's table was my mother and I. That was it. We talked to each other and made jokes between us, not our estranged cousins. Within a half hour of being there we were already making plans to leave. This side of the family made us feel uncomfortable, and they fucking loved every second of it. It's like the more they fed of our negative ass energy, the more *fabulous* they became. It was fucking nasty.

Either Momom had a enough of it or she was just ready to leave, because by the third time we begged to leave she was okay with it. We rushed to get our jackets and purses, the only person we actually stopped to say goodbye to was my Great Grandmother on my Momom's side. The angel she was slipped me 25$, kissing me on the cheek and telling me how much she missed me. I missed her, but right now my boyfriend Heroin was the one person I had to see.

But as much as I wanted to see him, I had to make a stop to someone more important on the way back to my apartment. My best friend's grave.

His mother got him the most beautiful stone. Purple, for his favorite color; it had his beautiful face and large smile on it. Right next to his name was his mother's. No if's and's or but's, she was getting buried next to her baby boy. Nobody would have a chance in hell to stop that.

I plopped myself down Indian style right in front of his headstone, lighting two cigarettes, one for me, one for him. I kissed my index and middle finger, then touched the picture his mother had attached to a metal stick that stuck in the ground. This was the only time I ever had with him anymore, and my mother and Momom patiently waited in the Malibu for me.

"How did I ever get like this, Ryan? Remember when I couldn't handle my weed? Or what about the time after we broke up and I took all those kpins and fell asleep all over Burger King's parking lot? Remember the time at Taco Bell when you taught me how to ride your BMX bike? You held the handles and wouldn't let go until I finally got the hang of it, clapping like a proud dad?"

I stole a glance over at Momom's car. My mother was sobbing into Momom's arms. I got angry, throwing my hands up in the air in a *'why is this bitch crying'* way. Momom simply shrugged her shoulders, patting the top of my mother's auburn colored head.

"I'm literally fucking tortured every day, Ry. I wake up sick, David starts the mental abuse parade, and I'm trying my hardest not to go to work sick. Life sucks and that's it, I guess. God won't even kill me. Can you believe that? I literally am begging him to kill me all the time and here I am, talking to you from the grave rather than in heaven."

It wasn't like me to notice time pass by so quickly. Every second of my life always seemingly ticked by, waving hello as they fell off the surface to make room for the next one. But for some reason here I am, crying to my dead best friend because the last two years passed by with such a strong blur that it made my head dizzy. I could no longer recall exact moments of my life, moments I promised myself I would put in my book had I ever made one. I could no longer remember specific outfits of when I got arrested or when I got robbed or when something kinda okay happened. In my head, it may have been 2012, but in reality it was 2014. Two years passed just like that, thanks to heroin. I had so quickly lost control of my life that my brain just couldn't catch up.

I looked over to my mother again, who was still sobbing, then back to Ryan's face.

Ryan just wanted so badly to silence his demons. He so badly just wanted to make them all quiet and live his life that he would do anything to make that reality true. He wanted to feel *good,* mentally. When mental was done, the physical part took over - the part nobody can deny. He lost control, too. Something he so badly wanted, he lost completely. I lost completely. While trying to silence my demons, I lost. People are congratulating me for being so strong for all the shit I went through and I am just not. Strong people do not lose.

"Please help me." I was crying now and didn't care who saw it. *"I want to die. Please help me because I can't help myself anymore. Everybody knows and they won't confront me because they're scared I'll fully disappear. My family hates me. I have no friends. Oh my god, Ryan, Please. Help me."*

I got up slowly, brushing strands of frozen grass off my yoga pants and walked back to the Malibu. "Why are you crying right now?"

My mom sniffled, the perfect dramatic addition to her act. "I just couldn't imagine if anything happened to you, Kayla! Don't be so rude!"

Momom placed an arm around my mom, awkwardly holding her as she drove the short distance from the cemetery to our beat apartment on Hamilton Ave. By the time we got to the first light at the Quik Chek, I must have rolled my eyes at the least 5 times. It was typical of her to make this all about her. She didn't even know Ryan. She didn't even know the fucking suffering I went through every day under her roof. She always tries to confront me with empty dope bags, but if she really cared, she'd send me to a fucking rehab or forbid David to ever step a dirty foot into our apartment again.

She never did though.

David was, of course, waiting at the apartment for us. The familiar sense of dread filled up my lungs as I trudged past him and went into my room. I began tearing up my room, throwing dresser drawer after dresser drawer to the dirty carpet in search of *something.* The other day, I hid a bag of some really weak stamp called *Scorpion.* According to David, he didn't touch it. The empty spot where it was placed safely begged to differ.

"I'm out," I said through gritted teeth. "I'm fucking DONE!"

David snorted. "What? Bad time at rich white family central?"

"Oh my god, no. Can you not right now? Please?" I didn't look at him as I snapped back, just ripped my clothes out of the closet as breakdown 2K14 began. When no dope magically appeared, I rampaged my way into the living room. My mother sat astonished as I ripped the green love seat cushions out of their spot. There had to be dope somewhere.

"What is she doing?!?"

"Have a mental breakdown, Laura," David said simply, going into my Betsey Johnson purse and stealing a Newport. "That's what happens when you're sick."

"I'm not fucking sick!" I screamed at the top of my lungs. I wasn't sick. I had just lost my fucking mind and didn't care anymore. Everything was finally coming to a surface, and I didn't care.

Jordan leaving and never coming back, David making me walk at 2 in the morning for cigarette butts; robbing money from whoever and stealing money off a Walmart credit card my Momom Taco Bell gave me. Losing my friends. Kyle overdosing. Shooting up heroin at 17. It all came to a disgusting head.

In the background, my mom began to sob. "Oh, here she goes. It's always about you, right? What about the night I walked 30 minutes in the freezing cold sick as a dog for your Adderall, huh? The night I had to lock myself in my room because you told me not to speak until I found Molly? You have no reason to cry right now. None."

Her sob lasted for about another minute, until she took a deep breath and calmed herself more than I have ever seen her. "Kayla. David. Please, put the cushions back and sit down."

David nodded his head at me, making me in return roll my eyes and shove the cushions back in place. I lit a cigarette, sitting down with my knees hugging my chest. Before my mother was able to speak, David cut her off.

"Laura, I'll give you 6 bucks to buy a stick for me tomorrow." A stick was a 3 mg Xanax. "I'm ready to finally try and get clean for real this time."

Before I even could think about what to say, my throat formed words for me. "I am too."

My head was in a haze, but before me David and my mother were figuring out how this was going to work. She would buy 3 sticks and give them to us throughout the next 3 days. She would make sure we were hydrated, and make sure to take care of us however she could while she was not working. She had Imodium on deck, she had Advil on deck; she would even help us pick up our skinny bodies to make it to the bathroom. She would make it as painless as possible.

David and I looked at each other, cerulean blues meeting hazel nothings. To David, this was a way to prove himself worthy enough to Marie. If he could stay clean, he would weasel his way into her heart. Fuck the two kids they shared, the same ones that Dyfs had; her pussy mattered more. Excuse my French.

But to me, I would really try. I would take Xanax piece after Xanax piece, hoping to sleep through the worst of the chills and vomit. I would make my mother feel like she could actually breathe in her own home. She wouldn't have to threaten me anymore. I nodded to David, a telepathic way of saying 'Don't fuck up', then told my mom I agree to her rules.

The rest of the night was uneventful. Around midnight David got restless and began his tirade, which ended in me walking around Hamilton Ave to find cigarette butts for him. He would be 'look out', aka looking around pretending he didn't know me so he wouldn't be embarrassed. I was tasked with the job of looking like the junkie, but at this point, I didn't really mind. This would be over in 3 short days.

Chapter Seventeen

The next morning arrived like a bull fighting a toreador. I was sick, I was hurting, and I was ready to die. Right on cue, my mother came to my side with a Xanax.

"You know I have to sniff this, right?" I didn't wait for her disgusted reply as I chopped the green bar into powder, then inhaled it through my nostril in record time. David followed my actions a few minutes later, and before I knew it I fell asleep on the mattress I put in the living room because it was cooler in there than my room. Xanax had that power. I wasn't an avid user, so the effects hit me just as hard as I needed it too. I was in a Xanax coma on a twin sized mattress, no sheet needed to cover it. No blanket needed to cover *me*. I wouldn't doubt if the paper straw was still up my nose.

12 hours passed, and I woke up forgetting where I was. I rubbed the sleep from my eyes, and it wasn't until I tried to stretch my legs that the dope sickness hit me again. "Mommy?"

"No, Kay." She said sternly. "That was your only one for the day."

I cursed to myself, taking my time to push myself off the mattress. I couldn't do this cold turkey. I stole a glance at David. His pale body was in fetal position on the loveseat, sweat dancing off his body like it had somewhere to be.

I rolled my eyes. We would NOT be able to do this.

I dragged myself to my room, pushing the door open with my shoulder and ignoring Cleo cat's meows of welcome. *Mom's alive, mom's alive!* No, baby. Mom's a zombie.

I made my way over to my bed and pushed the clothes off of it, just about giving up as bile threatened to make its way out of my mouth. Not yet. Not right now. I had scrapes that would get me through today. The first day is always the worst, and this would help..

I lifted the mattress up, taking the *American Horror Story* DVD case out and emptying its contents to the carpet. Meeting me were about three days worth of empty heroin bags, a paper straw, and a paper clip bent to stand straight. I preferred bic pens as straws since they were a lot more smoother, but paper straws held more residue.

I sat myself on the floor, beginning my ritual. Open the bag, scrape it with my ID, lick the glassine bag, try to make a line with whatever I could, then take the paperclip and meet the end with the inside of the straw. It was never enough to last me or make me as strong as I needed, but it was enough to get off E.

Somewhere between praying to God for a line longer than my pinky nail and crying to myself, I must have missed the sound of David's feet meeting the hallway floor. Before I knew it he was at my side, the DVD case in his hand.

"Give it back."

"What the fuck is this?" He demanded, bending down to pick up my straw.

I picked it up, now trying to take the case out of his hands without spilling any of the heroin. "It's my scrapes. I don't feel good. Do your own cotton."

He smirked, placing the DVD case on the ground. I hated that crooked smirk. It was a sign of the end of fucking times. "I want half."

"No."

"No?" His smirk disappeared, and before I had a chance to dive down and pick up my only chance of survival, he kicked it out from my reach. "No?! Do you want your fat fuck mom to know you're getting high?"

"It's just my fucking scrapes!" I cried, turning hysterical when I saw that my effort of getting well was futile. "THEY WERE JUST FUCKING SCRAPES!"

My mom showed up at this point, her eyes going wide at the scene before her. "What is this?!"

"Your junkie daughter was getting high," David said matter of factly, pointing at the scene before us.

"I was trying to get *well*. I won't be able to sleep tonight!"

"This is bullshit, Kayla. This is bullshit!" When my mother gets mad, her voice turns into a soprano yell. Like, it gets so loud and so high that she could fucking break a glass. I hated that voice.

"Why are you always taking his side?" I yelled back, my index finger shakily pointing to my ex boyfriend. "He wanted half of it! You know how hard this is and you just don't care!"

"You know what? Fine. I'm calling Momom, and kicking David out!" She ran into the living room to get her phone and we ran right with her.

"You can't kick me out!" David yelled, all the while I was leaning over my mother to get her phone.

"Mommy, please! Not Momom! Please!" My Momom was my angel. She was the only one who cared if I ate, if I was safe, or if my mom was treating me right. She was the light in the dark tunnel, and I could never have her hate me.

But my mother was not dope sick. She did not have a heroin addiction, and she was not trying to come off cold turkey like I was. She pushed me off her, my body meeting with cold hardwood and she opened the front door. "Get the FUCK out, David!"

"You can't make me get out, Laura." He said smug, placing his body in the middle of her and the entrance way. "You can't call the cops, you can't beat me."

"I can't beat you?!" The high shrill was back, and as she dialed my grandmother's number she squared her fists up. My fucking mother just squared up with David, women beater of the fucking century. Oh my god.

"No! No, no, no!" I shrieked, pushing my body between them.

Time moved slowly. Perhaps even more slow than when I had first begun this whole heroin addiction. I looked to my mom, who was towering over me and David. I glanced at her phone - she had finally called Momom. All the times she lied and said she was going to, she finally fucking did. 0:01; 0:02. On second 3, the light of my life answer. "Hello?"

This was it. I had to be quick. I had to be quiet.

I glanced back at David, whose fist was also now raised. If not for the severity of the situation, I'd probably laugh. Such a silly scene was playing out in front of me, and I had the unfortune of being in the middle. What a fucking life.

"Laura?" Momom's voice called on the other end.

Before my mother had a chance to respond, I turned my body to David. "It's fine, just stop I'll get money tom-"

"Kayla's doing heroin!"

And then I turned to my mother. My betrayer. The women who birthed me, left my life, then came back as my best friend like nothing had ever happened. I had to catch the breath that was practically knocked out of me. "Momom! Please! No!"

"She's been doing dope with David for the last few months, mom! Yup, *that's* where your money is going!"

"You gotta go," I quietly pleaded, pushing David's pale body to the apartment building's front door. "Just for now. Just 'till this blows over. Please."

He fought his way out of the door, but by the grace of God he did leave. I locked the door behind me, then tried to grab the phone out of my mother's hand. I was so weak that all she had to do was put her palm to my forehead to stop me. I was powerless. My life was over.

Throughout this whole journey, my biggest fear was NEVER my mother or even my father finding out. My mother had her ideas, she had her own suspicions. But to the best of my knowledge, my momom didn't and I wanted to keep it that way. Someone as angel like as her, someone who constantly tried to make sure my life was okay didn't need to go through the pain of having a heroin addict granddaughter. She already went through that with my mother; my aunt, her other daughter, was also an alcoholic. She needed *someone* normal.

I blocked out whatever my mom was saying, the words "my momom" coming out as a sob as I threw myself to the mattress on the ground.

"Yeah, only worry about your fucking momom. How typical." My mother sneered, sitting on the loveseat.

"Momom, oh momom. I'm so sorry my momom." I had to be in shock, because those were the only words that were capable of verbalizing out of my mouth. In fact, that's all I said for the next two days.

My mother had David's half of Xanax and gave it to me, each dose knocking me out for a good 12 hours. I had off work for the next 4 days from Shoprite so I was free to be in a Xanax induced coma. I only woke up to take more Xanax and cry. "Momom, I'm so sorry. My momom, momom, momom…"

By the 2nd day, my mother wasn't as mad at me. She was only hurt that I cried about momom, and not about hurting the women who birthed my 9lb my 5oz body. "Kay, please call her. Momom isn't mad at -"

Whenever I heard Momom's name, I started my sobs from the beginning. "My momom. I'm so sorry Momom. I'm so fucking sorry, Momom."

"Kay, please baby." A soft hand touched my shoulder, and I cried harder. "Why are you crying so hard? Momom's not mad at you! The only thing you should be crying about is how you're gonna get clean."

I didn't want to hear my betrayer talk anymore, so in between waiting for another dose of Xanax I got up and went to the bathroom. Before this mess, I got a box of Rihanna red Splat hair dye and Redken red shampoo. From being dope sick and working and searching the ground for cigarette butts, I never really had the time to dye my hair. Now was as good as time as any.

I calmed myself down and took out all the ingredients, laying them out in a neat line on the sink. First came the bleach, which burned my nose as I painted it on my brunette hair. I set the timer for an hour.

I checked my Facebook, ignoring the messages I got from David. Next to me, the shitty 25$ flip phone I got to replace my android chirped. A text message. I looked at the name and my heart skipped a beat. Momom.

'Kay, I love u and I am not mad at u. U r my whole world and -'

I couldn't read anymore because I was just so exhausted from crying. I didn't want to cry anymore, and to be honest I wasn't even sure if tears would come out. So I put my phone down and went to wash the bleach that was burning my scalp off, making sure to check regularly for any chunks of falling hair. After drying my hair I mixed the red in, painting it as best as I could. After doing my best, I set the timer for another hour. For the first time in 2 days, I finally talked to my mother.

"Does it look like I got it all?"

Excited that I was finally acknowledging her, she jumped up from her bed and ran to my side. After inspecting my hair, she nodded. "You did a good job! I can't wait to see it when you wash it out and dry it!"

All I could do was nod. I still wasn't in the mood to reconcile. For the next hour I chain smoked, noting how the Xanax coma must have made me miss the worst of my withdrawals because I didn't feel terrible. I was yawning here and there and had a terrible drippy nose, but I wasn't as bad as I should be. I counted my blessings and thanked God as cold water ran over my freshly dyed head.

After blow drying and straightening my hair and flexing for Facebook, I was ready to go to sleep. I had to finally bite the bullet and text Momom. She would be driving me to and from work in a day, and I had to get over the awkwardness now.

'I'm sorry. I never meant for any of this to happen. Please forgive me i love u and popop so so much.'

"Goodnight, Mommy. Love you." I didn't wait for her reply, though. Before I knew what was happening, I was asleep.

From that night.

Two nights after.

I awoke the next day to a phone in my face. Disgruntled, I pushed it away from me. It was shoved right back into its original spot.

"Kayla, it's *the* call! It's the intake lady from the clinic!"

Over the last 3 days, my mom and I (silently, may I add) agreed the best form of treatment would be New Horizons treatment center -

aka the methadone clinic in Trenton. Suboxone obviously didn't work, cold turkey was shit, and no matter what I did I just always wanted to get high. Methadone would block my receptors, making the want to get high a thing of the past. For the past 7 years my mother herself was on the clinic. Shit, before a year ago my dad was on and off the program for the same amount of time. Thanks to methadone, they would both probably be dead. The negative stigma around it never bothered me, and because I was raised around it I knew the truth; I knew it was a miracle.

"Hello?" The female voice over the phone had a hint of annoyance, no doubt due to my mother calling every day the last few days, 3 times daily.

"Uhm, yeah. Hi. My name is Kayla Small. Uhm, I wanna start the program."

"How long have you been using heroin?"

My mother looked at me, her eyes turned into slits. Well, this was it. "About two years. Maybe a little more. I dunno."

The yelling from my mother never came, though. She just continued to wait anxiously over the phone. "Intravenous?"

"No. Just snorting." That one time didn't count. It wasn't important.

"Okay." Typing. A lot of it. "When was the first time you began using drugs?"

"What? I don't know, I just told you like 2 years ago."

"No." Her voice was pure annoyance now. "Your first substance."

"Oh, uhm. Well, I got drunk at a wedding one time. I was like, 13. Then I started drinking 40's."

"40's of malt liquor?"

"40's of like, Olde E."

I could practically hear the eye roll in her sigh. "How many bags of heroin a day do you use?"

Again, I looked at my mother. If she didn't yell at me before, she sure as hell would now. "2 bundles a day. So around 20 bags. On a bad day it's only 5."

The yelling never came, though. "Okay, give the phone to your guardian, please."

My mother's freckled arm reached over at that point, taking her phone back and off of speaker phone. "Yes? This is her mother."

I didn't pay attention to what she was saying because I was *sick*. Full on dope sick. There were no Xanax left, no Klonopin. Just a shitty Valium that would prove effortless in the steps of the superior Xanax. The superior benzo.

"Okay, Kay. Todays Monday. On Wednesday you have your appointment at 6:30 in the morning. Will you be okay?" Her voice was so hopeful. It was so pure that I wanted to lie to her.

"I feel like crap." I didn't like to curse in front of her. "I don't know how long I can go, Mommy. But I'll try, okay?" Cue the sheepish smile.

I went to get ready for work after that. Slowly putting on yoga pants and all but crying as I slid the ugly Shoprite apron over my head. It'd be a miracle if I could last the whole work day. My phone went off next to me. Momom was around the corner.

I kissed my mother goodbye, she was no longer my betrayer but my actual mother again. I gave her my best smile, not only trying to convince her but myself that I can do this. That I would be okay.

Momom was there waiting, a smile on her beautiful face as I slowly stepped into the vehicle. My bones cracked, and I bit my lip to hold back a sob. "Hi, baby!"

"Hi, my momom." Don't sob, don't sob.

The ride wasn't awkward, or scary, or really anything besides normal for that matter. Momom made it perfect, and I was ashamed that I even thought she'd bring anything up. She was my hero, my light. She wouldn't do that to me even if I deserved it.

All too soon I got to Shoprite. All too soon I clocked in and went to my cash register lane with my till, wiping cold sweat off my lip as I prayed to God that someone would bomb the fucking place. I placed my phone inside my pocket and was met with a crisp, paper material. I pulled it out and wanted to cry. 20 fucking dollars. I wouldn't have to be sick for the next two days if I played my cards right, I wouldn't-

"Are you open?" Someone asked, taking me out of my thoughts. I looked up to the number '13' sign that wasn't lit up and sighed. I am now.

What seemed like an eternity later passed and I finally grew the balls to check the time. I had a mini panic attack when it was only two fucking hours later. I had to get out. Now. It was time to be the best fucking actress this shithole grocery store ever saw.

I saw the lady who would play the part with me, unknowingly of course. A sweet old lady with hair that just reached her shoulders, she would remember this grocery trip for awhile.

I smiled at her and she brought her cart to the register and I began. *Cough, cough.* Disgusting, pneumonia sounding coughs began to escape my lips as I turned my body around to cover them. The old lady gasped. "Oh, hunny! You don't sound good at all!"

"No," I croaked out, faking another cough as I rang up her items. "I'm scared I have bronchitis. I wasn't allowed to call out."

"Weren't allowed? No, unacceptable!" She was feeding into my act perfectly. "I'm going up there. Don't worry, I won't get you in trouble. But I won't leave until they send you home!"

I thanked her profusely, now ringing up her items at record speed. Shoprite had a tendency to be strict, but if a valued customer was saying something they HAD to send me home. At the end of her paying, she touched my hand. "Get ready to be sent home. Feel better, angel." And with a wink, she was off.

Within 5 minutes of my continued charade, someone who worked the front podium came up and took control of my register. "Alright, go home. We can't have you coughing to death."

I didn't wait for the OK from anyone else. Instead, I just called Momom to pick me up as I clocked out and hid my face from anyone to stop me. A few minutes later she arrived, knowing damn well I was dope sick but not saying anything in worry I'd go out and get high. I touched the 20$ in my apron. *Sorry, Momom.*

As I was coming around the block, I texted D and asked him to deliver 5 bags. I would lie and say Greg was picking me up to get my mind off of being sick. My mom would appreciate it.

I walked through the door and my mother rushed to my side to hug me. "Sorry, mommy. I just couldn't last."

"Baby, don't be sorry. No one is mad at you!" She exclaimed as she slipped me a Valium. "Lay down and -"

"I'm going out," I stated quickly, going to my room to throw my apron off. "I'm just driving around with Greg for a few."

"Well, okay.." She responded quietly. "I wish you would lay down, but if you think that'll help.."

"I'll be back, Mommy. Love you." I left the apartment and hid in the alley next door so she wouldn't see me. 15 minutes later D arrived, making it perfect time to say I was back from hanging out with Greg at Dunkin' Donuts. I walked inside and went to the bathroom, placing aside two bags that would have to last me until Wednesday. I did the other 3 right off the bat, not worrying about if my mom heard me because I could just blame it on my regular runny nose. I threw away all the evidence and went to the living room, cuddling up on the couch as I lit a cigarette.

Just two days. I could do it. I would be a whole new person in two short days. I think I'm really ready. I think the other day was finally my rock bottom.

Chapter Eighteen

Wednesday was here and I was *excited*. The night before I got a bundle of dope and my mom *let me*. To get on the clinic you had to have a dirty urine, and to her I hadn't done heroin in about 5 days. I needed the bundle for a good cause.

Obviously, I didn't fucking mind.

At 6 on the dot we left for the bus stop a few blocks down from the apartment. At 6:15 the bus came, and my mother practically threw the money at the driver. To this day, I think she was more excited than I was. Her one and only daughter was getting clean. Her pride and joy would be getting help and would be the sweet girl she once was.

I was never gone, though. Heroin just gave me a new face. Heroin gave me the confidence to rob people and not think twice. Heroin was so powerful it silenced the down to earth Kayla. Would methadone bring her back out again? Would methadone make me repent? Well, I guess we would find out.

We got off the bus in downtown Trenton and walked the short distance to the clinic. We passed pawn shops and the community college; we passed drug addicts that I was convinced didn't look a thing like me. They did, though. Same sunken eyes, gray skin and hollow cheeks. The only difference was that a majority of them were homeless. I was getting clean just before that point in my life.

We finally arrived to New Horizon Treatment Center. A large red brick building surrounded by iron wrought fences, it intimidated me. I remember coming here as a child with my mother - a time that seemed so long ago in my memories. Back then I had no reason to fear this building. But now, it was my last fucking chance.

We went to the red painted door all the way to the left and climbed what seemed to be a hundred steep steps. When we got to the waiting room my mother signed me in.

"Are you okay? Did the bags you do this morning help?" My mom whispered as she brought me into a tight embrace.

I nodded. "Yes, mommy." Two bags was *nothing* compared to what I needed daily, but it got me off E and I wasn't sick. I couldn't complain, especially since I didn't even buy the dope.

After what seemed like an eternity, the lady who asked me the questions over the phone brought me into the back. My anxiety rose through my chest as she had me sit across from her, her wooden desk the perfect barricade. A computer sat in front of her, and the webcam that sat on top starred at me. "Okay, what's your name and how old are you?"

I took a deep a breath before answering. "Kayla Small. I'm, uh, 19."

"How tall are you and how much do you weigh?" When she saw my shrug, she spun her chair so she was facing me. "I need a guesstimate here."

"Like, 5'6 maybe? And I don't know, 'prolly like 120."

"What other drugs are you using besides heroin?"

"Just the occasional Xanax."

"How many times a week? How many milligrams?"

The need for exact answers took me back. "Uhm.. I don't know. Sometimes twice a week. But usually only like, 5 times a month. No more than 3 milligrams, though."

"And when did you begin crack?"

"Excuse me?" Not even my mother knew about the one time I smoked crack, and that was about a week and a half ago! I didn't take a drug test yet, but even if I did it wouldn't show up. Scared that my mother would somehow find out, I lied. "I've never done crack."

"You have to forgive me, Kayla." The way she said my name made it sound like 'Kala.' I hated that. "About 90 percent of people on this program have, or still do, participate in smoking crack. Anyway, you said the first substance you did was drink. What age were you then?"

The questions continued for a good 15 minutes and ended after she took my client photo and gave me a number. I was given instructions to tell the dosing nurse every morning that number, but if I somehow forgot they could look my name up. I made it a point to never forget.

According to the intake lady, whose name turned out to be Diane, I had been a drug user since I was 13 - the first time I ever got drunk at that wedding with my dad. I tried to fight with her, and explain I only became a drug user when I first started heroin, but that didn't matter. Apparently, it starts when you do your first mind altering substance. That made me feel worse about myself.

When I was done I walked back down the steep stairs with my mother and went outside to go through another door, this time the one farthest right. This is where I would go every day to get dosed and take my weekly urine. I sat inside the waiting room, trying to be patient while I waited for my name to be called. First came the drug test, then the physical, then my first dose of methadone. During my physical they took my height and weight, then they took my blood, gave me a TB test, and an EKG test to make sure my heart was okay. I was an inch and ten pounds lighter than I told Diane, but at least my heart was good. The only nerve wrecking thing was the fact that I had to wait for my blood test results. 4 whole days I had to worry about if I had Hep-C or if heroin had ruined my liver or something crazy like that. For a hypochondriac like myself, that was terrifying.

But I had no time to worry, because shortly after being poked and prodded it was time for me to get my dose. Instead of waiting in line, however, I was directed to the back to talk to the director of nursing.

"Welcome to New Horizons! My name is Deadra. You won't see much of me, but today we're going to figure out your dose and where you should stop to see how you feel, okay?" She waited for my response, and when I nodded she continued. "Like every patient, you'll start at 30 and continue to go up 10 a day. For someone who was doing two bundles of heroin a day, I suggest we stop you at 100 milligrams. Does that sound good to you?"

I could only nod my head again. This was too much information to comprehend, and I didn't really understand how milligrams worked with methadone. I got confused anyone converted heroin *bags* to fucking kilos or balloons.

"Okay! Great! Judy? 11029's dose, please."

An older lady with a cane and a posh spice haircut whom I would grow to love as one of my own family members came walking in, a plastic cup of water in one hand and a plastic cup of red liquid in the other. She handed it to me and tried her best to smile, but the look on her face was obvious: another wasted youth. She wasn't wrong.

I was on my way after that, my mother beaming with happiness as she introduced me to her friends who all smiled and congratulated me for coming on the program. Some of them looked worse than me, some of them looked like professionals who you'd see in the fucking government. It just proved the same thing: that addiction will never discriminate. Ever. It never fucking has and it never will. It will kidnap anyone it can get it's dirty, grimy hands on and won't think twice.

When I got back to my apartment I was still sick and did the rest of my dope, getting one of the best high's I ever had in my short life. It was clear to me now why my mother stressed that it wasn't a fucking game. I could easily stay on 30 milligrams for the rest of my addiction so I could still get high but still be well. If I didn't get money it wouldn't matter because the methadone would take away my sickness. I would be fucking invincible, right?

But I shook those thoughts away from my head. That wasn't the life I was ready to live. In 3 days, 1 shorter than I was originally told, I got all my test results back. I had no diseases. Everything was completely, 100% normal.

My name is Kayla Small. I'm 19. I am ready to no longer be a heroin addict.

Chapter Nineteen

I would like to say after that day I was clean, but that just isn't true and this is a memoir, after all. It took me awhile to get my dose right, 100 milligrams wasn't enough. I would still sometimes wake up sick and still want to get high - that just was not normal. Months after grueling fucking months were spent crying and fighting and figuring out *why*? Why wasn't this fucking working for me? Why wasn't I normal like everyone else?

I also fell asleep. A lot. I remember so clearly looking at everyone nodding out on methadone as a 'junkie', but that was not the case as I soon came to learn. I, and most of them, were falling asleep because our dose wasn't high *enough*. We fell asleep because our bodies finally got relief after taking our dose in the morning that all it wanted to do was recoup.

Finally, after months of fighting the clinic, my dose got normalized. 110 has kept me clean for 3 and a half years, and yes I mean clean. You are, 100 and 10 fucking percent, clean if you are on methadone. Do not let anyone tell you otherwise. Do not ever doubt yourself.

I don't talk to a lot of the people in this book anymore. Brian was, up until about 6 months ago, still shooting up. I deleted him off Facebook, but last time I checked he was clean. His old girlfriend Christina is clean, and so is Brenda. John has a child now, but I only know that through Facebook pictures. We haven't talked in about 2 years. Cristine is fighting for her life in a coma due to some piece of shit loser bashing her head in randomly, but through a recent update via Facebook she's doing a lot better. Marie lives in Florida. She now has 3 kids with David - 2 of which live with a foster family, one of which lives with her. David hasn't seen either of them since I was probably still using, honestly.

I don't know what's going on with David, and prefer to keep it that way. It's been like that for about 2 years. I assume he's still getting high. Jordan came back one day randomly after he went missing again for a literal year. We talked for a few weeks, then he got mad I was trying to get into another relationship. He called me a junkie for being on methadone, and tried to make fun of me for not doing it cold turkey like him. I recently just heard he relapsed and is now in Florida. My nickname isn't Karma for nothing, huh?

Viktoriya has recently added me back on Facebook. She gave me full permission to add her real name to this memoir, but I still refuse. She says she's clean, living in North Carolina with a nice man with 2 children (I think.) I hope she is. Jess was released from jail, and about a year and a half later went back. A few days ago she got 5 years. I try to write her once a week.

I'm engaged to the love of my life, who I actually met at the clinic a few months in. His name is Joseph.

It was a Saturday, and I went in the morning with my mom's friend to feed the stray cats and get my take home bottle. As I was leaving the dosing nurse's station, a boy pacing around the waiting room caught my eye. He looked familiar, and because I was still working at Shoprite I convinced myself that was where I knew him from. "Do you work at Shoprite?"

He just shook his head, his curly ponytail bouncing as he did it. I paid no mind until a few days later he commented on my status, and I realized I recognized his unique features from a fucking social media platform. After that comment, the rest was history. The first time we ever talked on the phone I ran inside to tell my mother I just met my baby's father.

Our relationship was difficult, perhaps if it was easy we wouldn't be together now. We ignored each other a lot, and more times than not we fought. But something about Joseph always kept me needing more. Maybe it was those dimples - those fucking dimples that take my breath way even now. Or maybe it was just him: the way he fought for us, the way he wanted us to work. Whatever it was worked, because he wrapped me into his fucking web and I will never tear myself down. He also has 3 years clean, thanks to hard work and methadone.

I'm writing because it is so fucking important to know that addiction HAPPENS. It happens to anyone, at anywhere, at anytime. If you told me 5 years ago on that hot August day that I would become addicted to heroin, I would never believe you. I knew damn well that the gene was in me, but I was stubborn and thought I was above it all.

I wasn't. YOU aren't. No one is above addiction and I cannot stress that enough. Through pure fucking determination I made it through. I'm one of the lucky ones. My fiancé, my mother, my father - we are all one of the lucky ones. It is only the 2nd week of September 2017, and more than 6 people I personally know have overdosed. There is help.

As for me, I just turned 22. I just got my GED and got accepted into an online veterinary technician college. I lost count after about 15 tattoos, and I like to think I'm the funniest person on the entire planet. Joseph is going to school to be a drug and alcohol counselor, and I have high hopes that he's going to be the best one yet.

There was a lot that didn't go in this book. I never really got into detail about what it's like to be dope sick, or how my 2 days of community service went. I felt that only the most important events belonged in here, some with photographic proof and some without. Maybe one day I'll write a second memoir. Hopefully it won't be as shitty as this one, right?

My story is not over, and yours isn't either. There is hope. There is help.

Thank you for reading my memoir. My name is Kayla Small, and I am a recovering addict.

Joseph and I's first picture. October 2015.

My mother and I, about a week into the clinic.

30 days on program.

"I Am More Than A Junkie" - Kayla Small.
My name is Kayla. I'm a wife. I'm a daughter. I'm a full time worker. I'm mother to two cats and a golden retriever with dwarfism. I am one of the biggest animal rights activists in the world, and I am a best friend. I am a granddaughter, and I am a great-granddaughter. I am many things.

But, most important to some - I am just a junkie.

I am just a junkie, or so Facebook and Twitter constantly remind me. I am reminded of how much of a piece of shit I am. I see people saying 'junkies' are losers, degenerate scums and that I chose to make my life this way. I disagree, but because I am a junkie I have no say; I have no opinion in any topic. I am lower than pond scum.

I am on a maintenance drug, so in fact I am worse than a junkie. Fellow 'junkies' make fun of me, too. Apparently I am not clean. I am not strong enough. I have no willpower. I try to argue, saying I have willpower and am strong enough or there would still be three bundles of heroin in my system; they disagree. They say it's the same thing.

I am more than just a junkie.

I am more than just a junkie because I get up every morning and do not get high on drugs, or high in general at that. I am more than just a junkie because I feel every emotion that courses through my body; I know what it is like to cry and actually feel the pain that made it happen. I am not a junkie because the term 'junkie' is wrong and outdated. Nobody in the entire planet deserves to be called a junkie.

I work a regular 40 hours a week, not including overtime. I provide what I can for my family. Every morning I feed two stray cat colonies and make sure they're warm and their shelters are up to my standards. I love every single person I meet, and try to make someone laugh, even if it is just once.

I am not a loser, I am not scum. I am a human being like every judgmental asshole in the world.

The word junkie is just that, a word. It is not a correct adjective for a human being who is struggling with drug addiction. We are drug addicts, helpless drug addicts who sometime take a little while to find a reason to get clean, and that is okay. I am not a junkie, but a recovering drug addict.

I am more than just a junkie because I am a human. I have made mistakes like every single person in the universe, but by no means am I a degrading word. I am more than that, and I always will be.

I am more than a junkie.

Made in the USA
Lexington, KY
28 October 2017